A Biography of
BENJAMIN FRANKLIN
THE HOUSE ON MILK STREET, BOSTON, MASSACHUSETTS, WHERE BENJAMIN FRANKLIN, CHILD OF DESTINY, WAS BORN ON JANUARY 17TH, 1706.
OLD SOUTH MEETING HOUSE ACROSS THE ROAD FROM THE FRANKLINS, WHERE BEN WAS BAPTISED THE DAY HE WAS BORN.
FATHER: JOSIAH FRANKLIN
MOTHER: ABIAH FOLGER FRANKLIN
AMONG THE MANY GREAT AMERICANS, BENJAMIN FRANKLIN STANDS OUT AS ONE OF THE FIRST AND GREATEST. BORN IN AN ERA OF FEAR - FEAR OF GOD, OF WITCHES, OF THE INDIAN-INFESTED FORESTS - HIS LIFE IS A STORY OF COURAGE. HE ADDED TO THE GLORY AND REPUTATION OF AMERICA NOT ONLY BY ESTABLISHING SOME OF HER GREAT INSTITUTIONS. BUT BY MAKING HER UNDERSTOOD AND RESPECTED IN OTHER LANDS. BENJAMIN FRANKLIN IS AMERICA FOR HE IS THE PERFECT EXAMPLE OF WHAT CAN BE DONE IN THIS LAND OF OPPORTUNITY BY ANYONE WHO HAS THE DESIRE AND DETERMINATION TO SUCCEED.

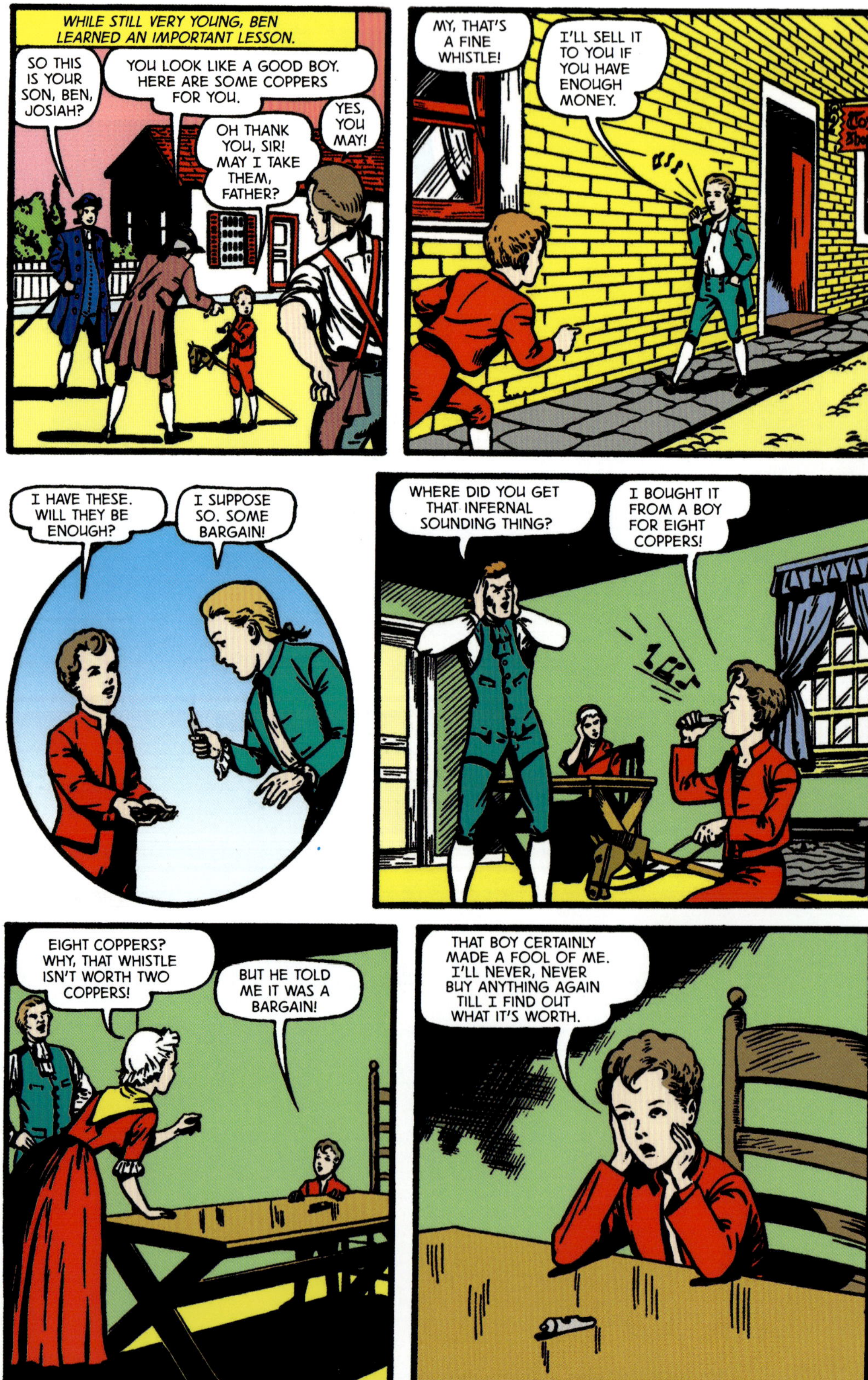
WHILE STILL VERY YOUNG, BEN LEARNED AN IMPORTANT LESSON.
SO THIS IS YOUR SON, BEN, JOSIAH?
YOU LOOK LIKE A GOOD BOY. HERE ARE SOME COPPERS FOR YOU.
OH THANK YOU, SIR! MAY I TAKE THEM, FATHER?
YES, YOU MAY!
MY, THAT'S A FINE WHISTLE!
I'LL SELL IT TO YOU IF YOU HAVE ENOUGH MONEY.
I HAVE THESE. WILL THEY BE ENOUGH?
I SUPPOSE SO. SOME BARGAIN!
WHERE DID YOU GET THAT INFERNAL SOUNDING THING?
I BOUGHT IT FROM A BOY FOR EIGHT COPPERS!
EIGHT COPPERS? WHY, THAT WHISTLE ISN'T WORTH TWO COPPERS!
BUT HE TOLD ME IT WAS A BARGAIN!
THAT BOY CERTAINLY MADE A FOOL OF ME. I'LL NEVER, NEVER BUY ANYTHING AGAIN TILL I FIND OUT WHAT IT'S WORTH.

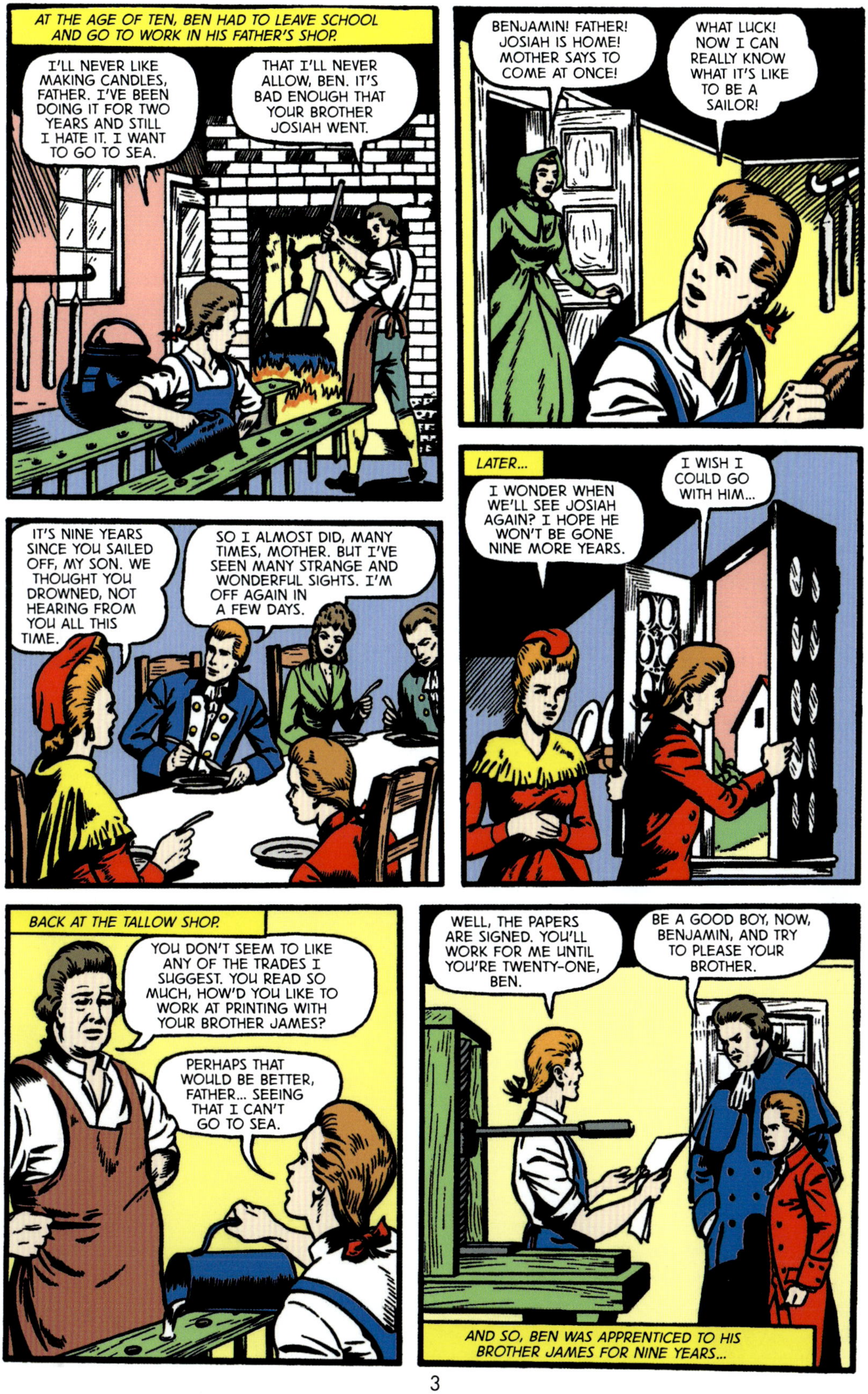
AT THE AGE OF TEN, BEN HAD TO LEAVE SCHOOL AND GO TO WORK IN HIS FATHER'S SHOP.
I'LL NEVER LIKE MAKING CANDLES, FATHER. I'VE BEEN DOING IT FOR TWO YEARS AND STILL I HATE IT. I WANT TO GO TO SEA.
THAT I'LL NEVER ALLOW, BEN. IT'S BAD ENOUGH THAT YOUR BROTHER JOSIAH WENT.
BENJAMIN! FATHER! JOSIAH IS HOME! MOTHER SAYS TO COME AT ONCE!
WHAT LUCK! NOW I CAN REALLY KNOW WHAT IT'S LIKE TO BE A SAILOR!
IT'S NINE YEARS SINCE YOU SAILED OFF, MY SON. WE THOUGHT YOU DROWNED, NOT HEARING FROM YOU ALL THIS TIME.
SO I ALMOST DID, MANY TIMES, MOTHER. BUT I'VE SEEN MANY STRANGE AND WONDERFUL SIGHTS. I'M OFF AGAIN IN A FEW DAYS.
LATER...
I WONDER WHEN WE'LL SEE JOSIAH AGAIN? I HOPE HE WON'T BE GONE NINE MORE YEARS.
I WISH I COULD GO WITH HIM...
BACK AT THE TALLOW SHOP.
YOU DON'T SEEM TO LIKE ANY OF THE TRADES I SUGGEST. YOU READ SO MUCH, HOW'D YOU LIKE TO WORK AT PRINTING WITH YOUR BROTHER JAMES?
PERHAPS THAT WOULD BE BETTER, FATHER... SEEING THAT I CAN'T GO TO SEA.
WELL, THE PAPERS ARE SIGNED. YOU'LL WORK FOR ME UNTIL YOU'RE TWENTY-ONE, BEN.
BE A GOOD BOY, NOW, BENJAMIN, AND TRY TO PLEASE YOUR BROTHER.
AND SO, BEN WAS APPRENTICED TO HIS BROTHER JAMES FOR NINE YEARS...

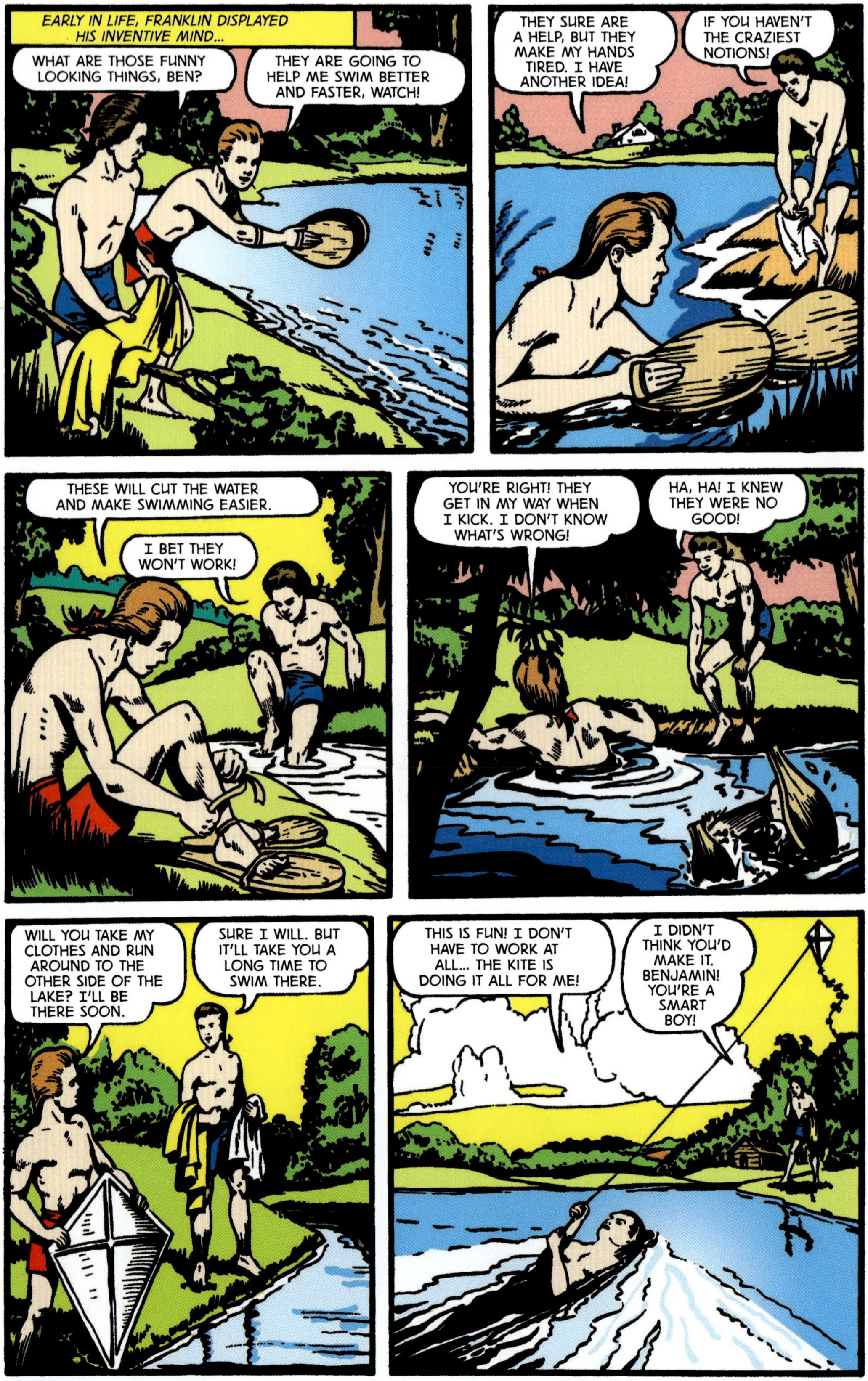
EARLY IN LIFE, FRANKLIN DISPLAYED HIS INVENTIVE MIND...
WHAT ARE THOSE FUNNY LOOKING THINGS, BEN?
THEY ARE GOING TO HELP ME SWIM BETTER AND FASTER, WATCH!
THEY SURE ARE A HELP, BUT THEY MAKE MY HANDS TIRED. I HAVE ANOTHER IDEA!
IF YOU HAVEN'T THE CRAZIEST NOTIONS!
THESE WILL CUT THE WATER AND MAKE SWIMMING EASIER.
I BET THEY WON'T WORK!
YOU'RE RIGHT! THEY GET IN MY WAY WHEN I KICK. I DON'T KNOW WHAT'S WRONG!
HA, HA! I KNEW THEY WERE NO GOOD!
WILL YOU TAKE MY CLOTHES AND RUN AROUND TO THE OTHER SIDE OF THE LAKE? I'LL BE THERE SOON.
SURE I WILL. BUT IT'LL TAKE YOU A LONG TIME TO SWIM THERE.
THIS IS FUN! I DON'T HAVE TO WORK AT ALL... THE KITE IS DOING IT ALL FOR ME!
I DIDN'T THINK YOU'D MAKE IT. BENJAMIN! YOU'RE A SMART BOY!

BEN WORKED HARD FOR HIS BROTHER, BUT JAMES WAS DIFFICULT TO PLEASE...
THESE ARE FAIR POEMS YOU'VE BEEN WRITING! WHY DON'T YOU TAKE SOME OUT AND SELL THEM IN THE STREET?
I'M PRINTING SOME NOW. DO YOU REALLY THINK I COULD SELL THEM?
WHAT IS THIS, SON?
A NEW BALLAD, "THE LIGHT HOUSE TRAGEDY." ONLY SIX COPPERS, SIR.
NOTHING SEEMED TO PLEASE JAMES...
I'VE SOLD SIXTY COPIES OF THE "TRAGEDY"! ISN'T THAT WONDERFUL?
IF YOU DID MORE WRITING AND LESS READING, YOU'D BE BETTER OFF...
WHILE AT HOME...
THOSE VERSES OF YOURS ARE NONSENSE! YOU OUGHT TO BE ASHAMED OF YOURSELF FOR WRITING SUCH STUFF. I WANT YOU TO STOP IT!
ALL RIGHT, FATHER. I WON'T WRITE ANYMORE... BUT I DID SELL A LOT!
EVERY SPARE MOMENT WAS SPENT READING.
SOME BOOK! I HOPE I CAN FINISH IT IN MY LUNCH HOUR; I DON'T GET MUCH TIME TO READ...
QUARRELS WITH BROTHER JAMES WERE FREQUENT...
YOU ALWAYS THINK YOU KNOW BETTER! I'M RUNNING THIS SHOP!
BUT I ONLY WANTED TO HELP!

THE DAY FINALLY ARRIVED WHEN THE FRANKLINS BECAME PUBLISHERS. A NEW NEWSPAPER APPEARED.
UP GOES THE "NEW ENGLAND COURANT" TO DRY THE INKS...
JUST THINK, JAMES... IT'S ONLY THE FOURTH PAPER IN AMERICA!
THAT NIGHT...
The New England Courant
JAMES WON'T KNOW WHO WROTE THIS. HE'D NEVER PRINT IT IF HE REALISED I WAS "MRS DOGOOD!"
THIS ARTICLE BY MRS DOGOOD IS VERY GOOD!
YES, I WONDER WHO SHE IS?
IF THEY ONLY KNEW!
New England Courant
BUT JAMES EVENTUALLY FOUND OUT...
YOU DECEITFUL BOY! SO YOU WROTE THE DOGOOD PAPERS! I DON'T LIKE TO BE MADE A FOOL OF!
OUCH! I THOUGHT YOU'D BE PROUD OF ME!
BUT TROUBLE BREWED FOR JAMES.
TAKE MY ADVICE, JAMES STOP ATTACKING THE CLERGY AND MASSACHUSETTS COUNCIL IN YOUR PAPERS!
BAH! IT'S DOUBLED CIRCULATION!
AND THE STORM BROKE... THROWING JAMES IN JAIL...
I DIDN'T THINK THEY'D DO THAT TO JAMES. I WAS LUCKY TO GET OFF WITH JUST A SCOLDING!

THUS BEN BECAME A PUBLISHER... FOR AWHILE...
HELLO, JAMES! YOUR FOUR WEEKS ARE UP, I SEE.
HMM... BUT THEY WON'T LET ME PRINT THE "COURANT" ANYMORE...
WELL, JAMES, NOW THAT YOU'VE RETURNED BEN'S APPRENTICESHIP PAPERS, HE CAN PRINT THE PAPER!
YES, BUT THESE NEW PRIVATE PAPERS BIND HIM TO ME FOR SIX MORE YEARS.
AND SO THE BROTHERS RESUMED THEIR UNHAPPY BUSINESS RELATIONSHIP...
YOU INSOLENT BOY! I'LL TEACH YOU TO HAVE RESPECT FOR ME!
I ONLY WANTED TO SHOW YOU AN EASIER WAY TO DO IT!
MR FRANKLIN LISTENED TO BEN'S PROBLEM COOLLY...
YOUR BROTHER IS RIGHT, BEN. YOU'RE BOUND TO HIM AND THERE YOU'LL STAY!
BUT HE BEATS ME, FATHER. I DON'T WANT TO BE TREATED THAT WAY!
DETERMINED TO GET AWAY FROM JAMES, BEN APPLIED FOR WORK IN BOSTON...
I'LL WORK HARD FOR MY PAY, SIR!
YOUR BROTHER TOLD ME ABOUT YOU. GET OUT!
NO ONE WILL GIVE ME A JOB HERE; EVEN MY FRIENDS ARE AGAINST ME. I'M GOING TO TRY NEW YORK...

BEN LEFT BOSTON, THOUGH HE WAS STILL LEGALLY BOUND TO HIS BROTHER...
I'VE GOT TO GET TO NEW YORK, COLLINS. DO YOU THINK YOU COULD MANAGE IT FOR ME?
I THINK I CAN GET YOU PASSAGE ON A SLOOP. BUT YOU'LL NEED MONEY.
THAT NIGHT...
THIS IS THE BOAT, BEN. DID YOU GET THE MONEY?
YES, HERE IT IS. I SOLD SOME OF MY BOOKS TO GET IT.
PERHAPS I SHOULDN'T HAVE RUN AWAY. BUT I COULDN'T STAND IT... I DIDN'T HAVE A CHANCE!
BRADFORD PRINT SHOP, NEW YORK.
I THOUGHT I'D FIT IN WITH YOU, MR BRADFORD.
I HAVE NOTHING FOR YOU, BUT MY SON IN PHILADELPHIA MIGHT NEED A HELPER. WHY NOT TRY HIM?
THE TRIP THERE WAS A ROUGH ONE...
OOPS! THAT'S WHAT HE GETS FOR DRINKING TOO MUCH PUNCH. GRAB HIM, FRANKLIN!
ANYTHING CAN HAPPEN IN A STORM LIKE THIS!
DRAG THE BLOKE IN, MEN!
HELP! HIC...
AT AN INN IN BURLINGTON...
BUT I'M NOT A RUNAWAY SERVANT! I'M A PRINTER AND I'VE BEEN PROMISED A JOB IN PHILADELPHIA!
WELL, IF THAT'S THE CASE, SON, THERE'S A BOAT LEAVING FOR PHILADELPHIA TONIGHT!
THE BOY SPEAKS THE TRUTH, I BELIEVE.

PHILADELPHIA... AT AGE SEVENTEEN, BENJAMIN BEGAN A NEW LIFE...
AT LAST! I NEVER THOUGHT I'D MAKE IT! ONE DOLLAR LEFT AND AM I HUNGRY!
THAT BAKER CERTAINLY GAVE ME A LOT OF BREAD FOR THREE CENTS AND DOES IT TASTE GOOD!
WHAT A SILLY LOOKING BOY WITH ALL THAT BREAD!
HELLO, SON. JUST GOT IN FROM NEW YORK IN THE NICK OF TIME FOR THAT BOY FRANKLIN. THINK YOU CAN FIND SOMETHING FOR HIM TO DO?
NOT A THING, FATHER, BUT HE CAN TRY KEIMER, THE NEW PRINTER!
THANK YOU, MR BRADFORD!
ANDREW BRADFORD PRINTER
LATER... AT KEIMER'S PRINT SHOP...
THE PRESS IS WORKING AGAIN, MR KEIMER. SHE'LL PRINT ANYTHING, NOW!
YOU CERTAINLY KNOW YOUR JOB, BEN. BY THE WAY, I'VE ARRANGED FOR YOU TO LIVE WITH THE READ FAMILY!
I HOPE YOU'LL ENJOY LIVING IN PHILADELPHIA, BENJAMIN!
I'VE NEVER BEEN HAPPIER IN MY LIFE, MRS READ!

SEVERAL MONTHS LATER...
SO YOU'RE THE FRANKLIN I'VE BEEN HEARING ABOUT! I'M GOVERNOR KEITH AND THIS IS COLONEL FRENCH. I WOULD BE PLEASED IF YOU WOULD JOIN US AT THE TAVERN.
I AM HONOURED, SIR!
THE GOVERNOR THINKS HIGHLY OF YOUR WORK. HE SUGGESTS THAT YOU OPEN YOUR OWN PRINT SHOP!
BUT I HAVE NO MONEY!
PERHAPS YOUR FATHER WOULD HELP YOU. WHY NOT GO TO HIM?
AND SO, FRANKLIN RETURNED TO BOSTON... AND HOME...
BEN! YOU LOOK WONDERFUL, SON!
I'M SORRY TO REFUSE YOU, SON, BUT YOU'RE NOT OLD ENOUGH FOR A SHOP OF YOUR OWN.
GOVERNOR KEITH WILL BE DISAPPOINTED... AND SO AM I...
BACK AT THE GOVERNOR'S MANSION.
SIR, IT WOULD COST A HUNDRED POUNDS TO EQUIP A SHOP, AND MY FATHER REFUSES TO HELP...
I SUGGEST THAT YOU GO TO LONDON TO GET WHAT YOU NEED. I WILL GIVE YOU PAPERS TO ESTABLISH YOUR CREDIT.
SEVERAL DAYS LATER...
LONDON HOP
WE'D BETTER GO ABOARD, BEN. SHE'S DUE TO SAIL ANY MINUTE...
BUT WHERE IS THE GOVERNOR AND HIS LETTERS? HE PROMISED TO BE HERE!
THE CAPTAIN SAYS THERE ARE NO PAPERS FOR ME IN THE MAILBAGS, RALPH. WHAT SHALL I DO? I'VE BEEN BADLY DECEIVED...
I DON'T KNOW, BEN. THAT WAS A PRETTY MEAN TRICK OF THE GOVERNOR'S!

AS A RESULT OF GOVERNOR KEITH'S DECEPTION, BEN WAS STRANDED... BUT HE FOUND WORK AND REMAINED IN LONDON FOR TWO YEARS, SUPPORTING HIS FRIEND AS WELL...
I DON'T KNOW WHAT I WOULD HAVE DONE IF MR PALMER HADN'T GIVEN ME A JOB IN HIS PRINT SHOP...
YOU'RE JUST LUCKY, BEN. COULD YOU LEND ME TWO POUNDS...
LOOK AT HIM! CARRYING TWO TYPE FORMS AT ONE TIME!
THAT WATER YOU DRINK SURE IS STRONG!
YOU'D BE STRONG TOO IF YOU DRANK WATER INSTEAD OF BEER ALL THE TIME!
BUT OVERWORK AND HOMESICKNESS FINALLY GRIPPED FRANKLIN AND HE BECAME VERY ILL...
I WISH I COULD GO HOME AGAIN... IF I ONLY HAD THE TWENTY-SEVEN POUNDS RALPH OWES ME...
BORROWING MONEY FROM FRIENDS, BEN WAS SOON HOMEWARD BOUND...
WHAT DO YOU MAKE OF THAT? YOUNG FRANKLIN HAS SWUM ALMOST ALL THE WAY AROUND THE BOAT!
AMAZING! SAYS IT'S HIS WAY OF TAKING A BATH!
FUNNY, WHEN I WAS SICK, I NEVER THOUGHT I'D LOVE TO SEE AMERICA AGAIN. IT CERTAINLY LOOKS WONDERFUL TO ME... I WONDER HOW DEBORAH READ IS?
BACK AGAIN TO HIS OLD JOB AT KEIMER'S
THAT NEW MOULD YOU INVENTED FOR CASTING TYPE IS FINE, BEN. I'M SURE GLAD YOU CAME BACK FROM LONDON!
SO AM I. LUCKY I HAD FRIENDS FROM WHOM TO BORROW MONEY FOR MY PASSAGE.

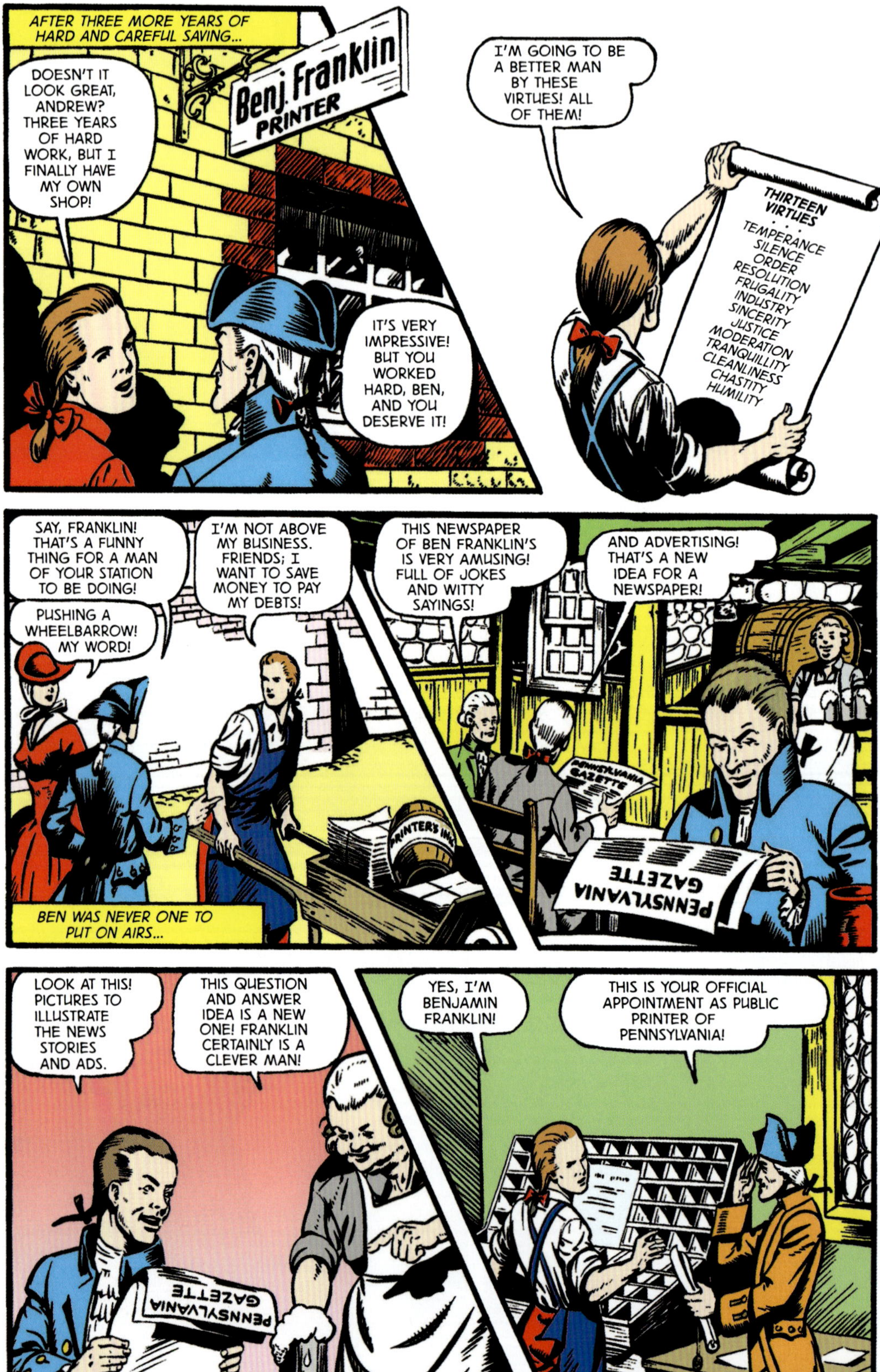
AFTER THREE MORE YEARS OF HARD AND CAREFUL SAVING...
Benj. Franklin PRINTER
DOESN'T IT LOOK GREAT, ANDREW? THREE YEARS OF HARD WORK, BUT I FINALLY HAVE MY OWN SHOP!
IT'S VERY IMPRESSIVE! BUT YOU WORKED HARD, BEN, AND YOU DESERVE IT!
I'M GOING TO BE A BETTER MAN BY THESE VIRTUES! ALL OF THEM!
THIRTEEN VIRTUES
TEMPERANCE
SILENCE
ORDER
RESOLUTION
FRUGALITY
INDUSTRY
SINCERITY
JUSTICE
MODERATION
TRANQUILLITY
CLEANLINESS
CHASTITY
HUMILITY
SAY, FRANKLIN! THAT'S A FUNNY THING FOR A MAN OF YOUR STATION TO BE DOING!
PUSHING A WHEELBARROW! MY WORD!
I'M NOT ABOVE MY BUSINESS. FRIENDS; I WANT TO SAVE MONEY TO PAY MY DEBTS!
PRINTER'S INK
BEN WAS NEVER ONE TO PUT ON AIRS...
THIS NEWSPAPER OF BEN FRANKLIN'S IS VERY AMUSING! FULL OF JOKES AND WITTY SAYINGS!
AND ADVERTISING! THAT'S A NEW IDEA FOR A NEWSPAPER!
PENNSYLVANIA GAZETTE
LOOK AT THIS! PICTURES TO ILLUSTRATE THE NEWS STORIES AND ADS.
THIS QUESTION AND ANSWER IDEA IS A NEW ONE! FRANKLIN CERTAINLY IS A CLEVER MAN!
PENNSYLVANIA GAZETTE
YES, I'M BENJAMIN FRANKLIN!
THIS IS YOUR OFFICIAL APPOINTMENT AS PUBLIC PRINTER OF PENNSYLVANIA!

...THEN, MARRIAGE...
WHEN WE ARE MARRIED, DEBORAH, YOU'LL FORGET ALL ABOUT YOUR PAST UNHAPPINESS!
MY FIRST MARRIAGE WAS A WRETCHED EXPERIENCE, BEN. BUT I'M SURE I COULD BE HAPPY WITH YOU.
WEDDING BELLS RANG OUT ON SEPTEMBER 1ST, 1730.
YOU HAVE CHOSEN A GOOD MAN THIS TIME, DEBORAH.
I KNOW, MOTHER, I KNOW!
LET'S GO AND DRINK TO THE HEALTH OF FRANKLIN AND HIS CHARMING BRIDE!
WITH HIS WIFE'S AID, FRANKLIN BECAME MORE AND MORE SUCCESSFUL...
THE BUSINESS HAS FLOURISHED IN THESE FEW YEARS, BEN.
YOU'VE BEEN A WORTHY HELPMATE, DEAR. I HAVE MANY PLANS FOR THE FUTURE.
THIS IDEA OF FRANKLIN'S FOR A CIRCULATING LIBRARY IS WONDERFUL!
JUST THINK... TO BE ABLE TO READ ALL THESE BOOKS IF YOU CAN'T AFFORD TO BUY THEM!
HE FOUNDED THE FIRST CIRCULATING PUBLIC LIBRARY...
HA, HA! THE GREATEST JOB FRANKLIN HAS DONE YET! "POOR RICHARD'S ALMANACK!"
IT'S A RIOT!
POOR RICHARD'S ALMANACK
AND THEN CAME ONE OF THE MOST FAMOUS PIECES OF LITERATURE EVER WRITTEN...
1733
POOR RICHARD'S ALMANACK
WORDS TO THE WISE
HE THAT DRINKS FAST PAYS SLOW.
THERE IS NO LITTLE ENEMY.
INNOCENCE IS ITS OWN DEFENCE.
HUNGER NEVER SAW BAD BREAD.
FOOLS MAKE FEASTS AND WISE MEN EAT THEM.
EAT TO LIVE. NOT LIVE TO EAT.

"SUCCESS" WAS FRANKLIN'S PARTNER FOR THE NEXT FEW YEARS...
DON'T TOUCH, WILLIAM! THE INK IS STILL WET.
DADDY'S PAPERS!
I SOLD ALMOST TEN THOUSAND ALMANACKS LAST YEAR AND THESE ARE EVEN BETTER!
IN 1736 FRANKLIN, AT THE AGE OF THIRTY, WAS APPOINTED TO HIS FIRST POLITICAL POST...
GREETINGS, BENJAMIN! WE'RE HERE TO TELL YOU THAT YOU'RE THE NEW CLERK OF THE PENNSYLVANIA ASSEMBLY!
I AM HONOURED, GENTLEMEN.
IN TIME, FRANKLIN BECAME POSTMASTER OF PHILADELPHIA...
Pennsylvania Gazette
THE POST OFFICE OF PHILADELPHIA IS NOW KEPT AT FRANKLIN'S ON MARKET STREET
I LIKE THIS JOB. BEING A POLICEMAN ISN'T SO BAD WHEN YOU GET PAID FOR IT. THANKS TO FRANKLIN.
HE ORGANISED PHILADELPHIA'S FIRST PAID REGULAR POLICE FORCE...
AND FORMED THE CITY'S FIRST VOLUNTEER FIRE EXTINGUISHING COMPANY...
IF IT WASN'T FOR YOU ORGANISING A VOLUNTEER FIRE EXTINGUISHING COMPANY, WE WOULD HAVE LOST EVERYTHING, MR FRANKLIN!
FIRE IS ONE OF THE GREATEST DESTROYERS. WE'VE GOT TO FIGHT IT!
IN 1742 CAME THE FRANKLIN STOVE...
THIS IS A GREAT STOVE, BEN! YOU OUGHT TO PATENT IT!
NO. I PROFIT BY THE INVENTIONS OF OTHERS; LET THEM PROFIT BY MINE!

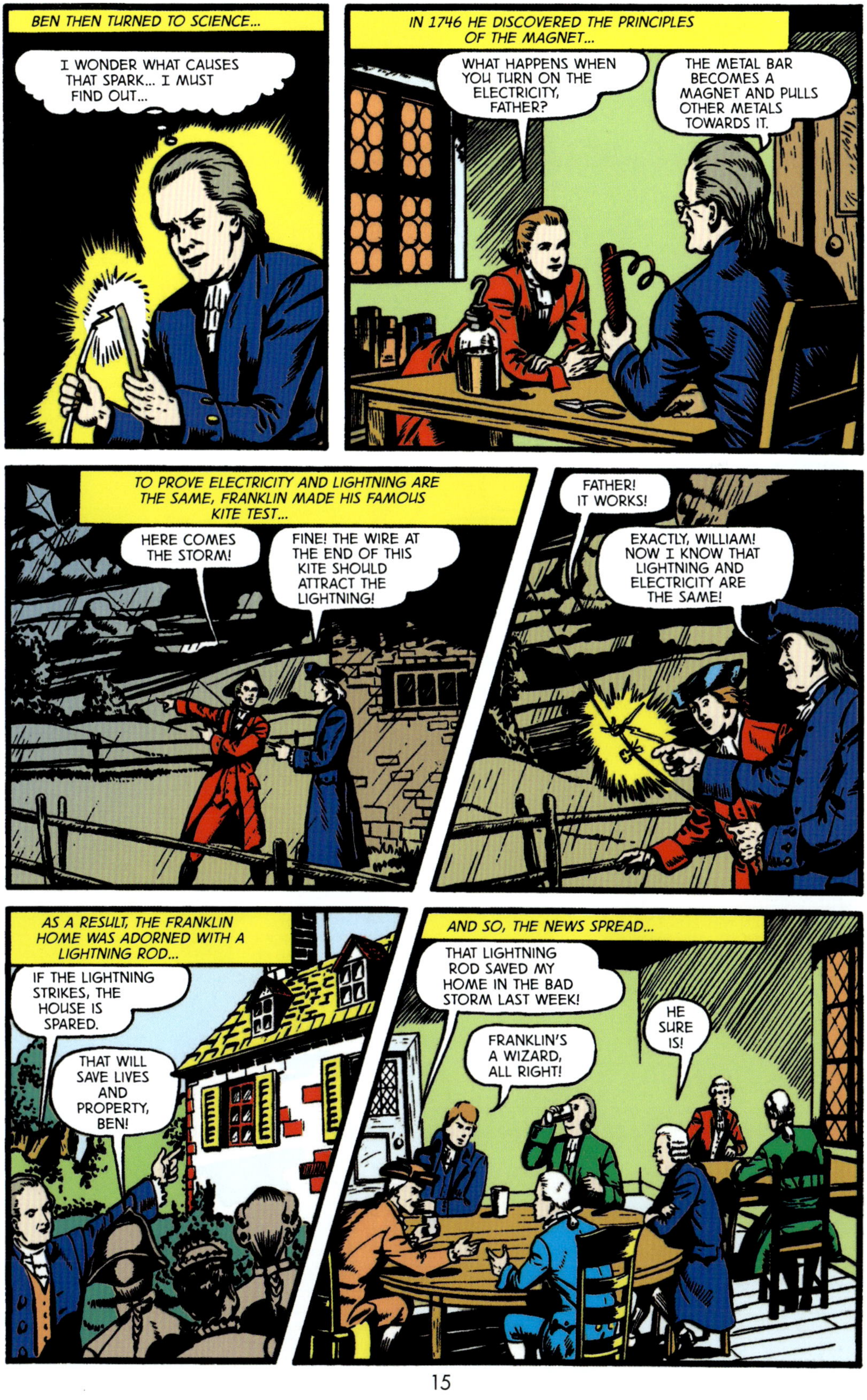
BEN THEN TURNED TO SCIENCE...
I WONDER WHAT CAUSES THAT SPARK... I MUST FIND OUT...
IN 1746 HE DISCOVERED THE PRINCIPLES OF THE MAGNET...
WHAT HAPPENS WHEN YOU TURN ON THE ELECTRICITY, FATHER?
THE METAL BAR BECOMES A MAGNET AND PULLS OTHER METALS TOWARDS IT.
TO PROVE ELECTRICITY AND LIGHTNING ARE THE SAME, FRANKLIN MADE HIS FAMOUS KITE TEST...
HERE COMES THE STORM!
FINE! THE WIRE AT THE END OF THIS KITE SHOULD ATTRACT THE LIGHTNING!
FATHER! IT WORKS!
EXACTLY, WILLIAM! NOW I KNOW THAT LIGHTNING AND ELECTRICITY ARE THE SAME!
AS A RESULT, THE FRANKLIN HOME WAS ADORNED WITH A LIGHTNING ROD...
IF THE LIGHTNING STRIKES, THE HOUSE IS SPARED.
THAT WILL SAVE LIVES AND PROPERTY, BEN!
AND SO, THE NEWS SPREAD...
THAT LIGHTNING ROD SAVED MY HOME IN THE BAD STORM LAST WEEK!
FRANKLIN'S A WIZARD, ALL RIGHT!
HE SURE IS!

1755... THE FRENCH AND INDIAN WAR... THE INHABITANTS OF PENNSYLVANIA WERE THREATENED BY VICIOUS INDIANS...
AND IN THE VILLAGE OF GNADEN-HUTTEN, 75 MILES FROM PHILADELPHIA, FRANKLIN WAS ASKED TO HELP...
THE INDIANS KEEP COMING. SOMETHING MUST BE DONE...
WE'LL ORGANISE A MILITIA AND BUILD FORTS!
WE MUST BE PROTECTED!
OUR LIVES ARE AT STAKE...
AND OUR CHILDREN!
RETURN TO YOUR HOMES. YOU WILL BE PROTECTED... DON'T FEAR!
YOU MEN WILL ELECT YOUR OWN OFFICERS AND ESTABLISH YOUR OWN COURTS!
THEN WE'LL WIPE, OUT THE FIGHTIN' REDSKINS!
FORWARD! THE PEOPLE MUST BE PROTECTED!
LET US MAKE HASTE!

FRANKLIN AND HIS MEN TOOK STEPS TO PROTECT THE COLONISTS...
YOU WILL BE STATIONED HERE TO CATCH ANY INDIANS LURKING ABOUT THREATENING THE VILLAGE.
YES, MR FRANKLIN! YOU CAN DEPEND ON US, SIR!
WE BUILT THE STOCKADE AND BROUGHT ARMS AND POWDER FROM NEW YORK AS YOU SUGGESTED, MR FRANKLIN.
GOOD!
AND I CAN STONE INDIANS FROM THE WALL!
THESE PEOPLE COME FROM ALL OVER. OUR FOOD IS ALMOST OUT AND ALL THEY DO IS DRINK AND QUARREL!
ORGANISE A PATROL, PARSONS, WITH YOU AS ACTING MAJOR. CLEAR AWAY THE BRUSH AND ORDER SENTINELS TO WATCH FOR INDIANS!
IN READING, PA, A TREATY WAS ARRANGED WITH FRIENDLY INDIANS...
INDIAN AND WHITE MAN FRIENDS, GOVERNOR MORRIS.
KEEP YOUR PROMISE, CHIEF, AND WE'LL KEEP OURS.
BUT...
WE THOUGHT YOU SHOULD HEAR WHAT THIS RUNNER HAS TO SAY, SIR!
THE SOLDIERS AT GNADEN-HUTTEN WERE TAKEN BY SURPRISE AND MASSACRED BY THE INDIANS, MR FRANKLIN!
WHAT! THE FRONTIER IS UN-PROTECTED!
YOU HAVE BEEN CHOSEN TO REBUILD THE FORT AND PROTECT THE PEOPLE, FRANKLIN!
THERE WILL BE A RICH REWARD FOR INDIAN SCALPS KILLED IN BATTLE, GOVERNOR!

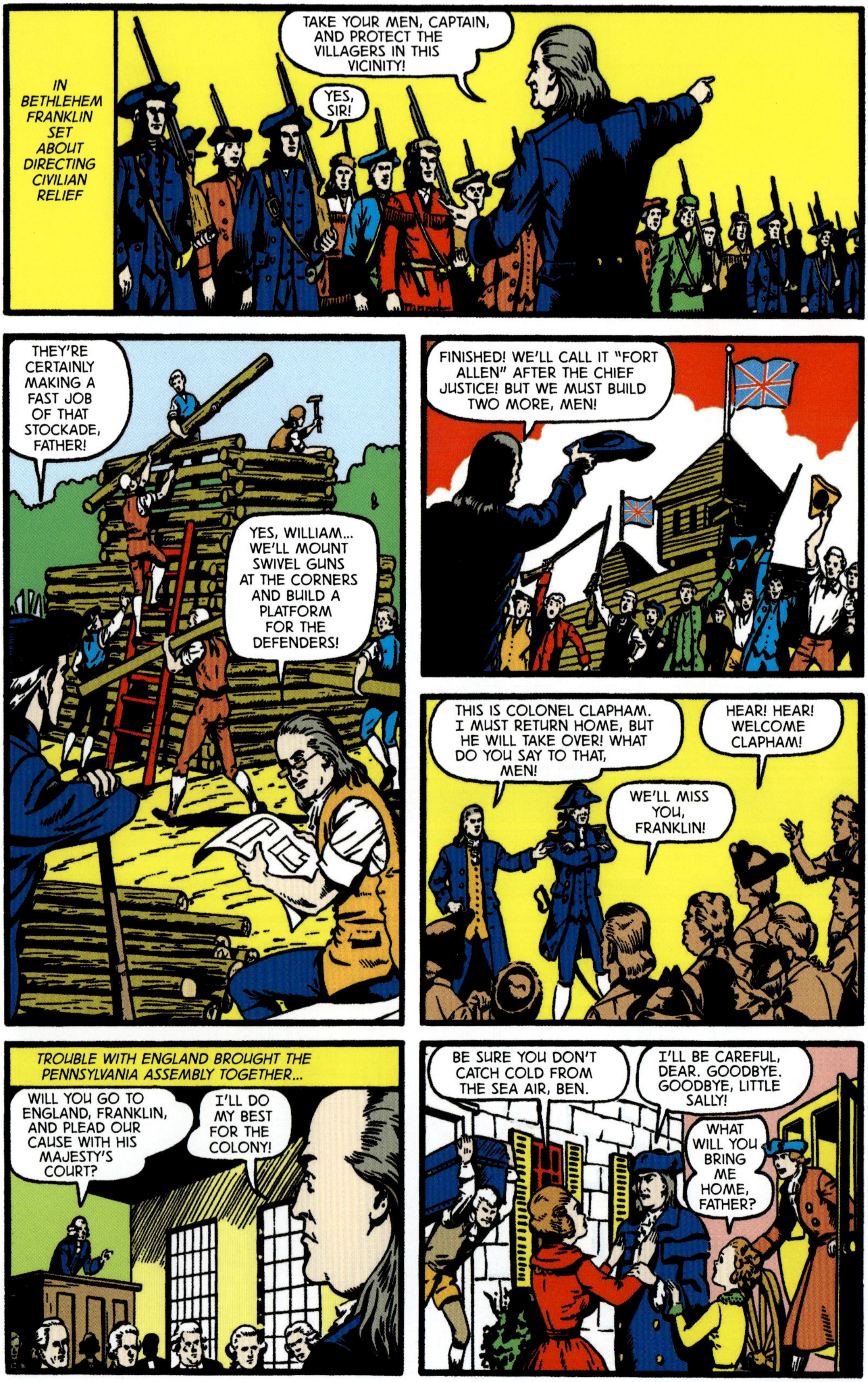
IN BETHLEHEM FRANKLIN SET ABOUT DIRECTING CIVILIAN RELIEF
TAKE YOUR MEN, CAPTAIN, AND PROTECT THE VILLAGERS IN THIS VICINITY!
YES, SIR!
THEY'RE CERTAINLY MAKING A FAST JOB OF THAT STOCKADE, FATHER!
YES, WILLIAM... WE'LL MOUNT SWIVEL GUNS AT THE CORNERS AND BUILD A PLATFORM FOR THE DEFENDERS!
FINISHED! WE'LL CALL IT "FORT ALLEN" AFTER THE CHIEF JUSTICE! BUT WE MUST BUILD TWO MORE, MEN!
THIS IS COLONEL CLAPHAM. I MUST RETURN HOME, BUT HE WILL TAKE OVER! WHAT DO YOU SAY TO THAT, MEN!
HEAR! HEAR! WELCOME CLAPHAM!
WE'LL MISS YOU, FRANKLIN!
TROUBLE WITH ENGLAND BROUGHT THE PENNSYLVANIA ASSEMBLY TOGETHER...
WILL YOU GO TO ENGLAND, FRANKLIN, AND PLEAD OUR CAUSE WITH HIS MAJESTY'S COURT?
I'LL DO MY BEST FOR THE COLONY!
BE SURE YOU DON'T CATCH COLD FROM THE SEA AIR, BEN.
I'LL BE CAREFUL, DEAR. GOODBYE. GOODBYE, LITTLE SALLY!
WHAT WILL YOU BRING ME HOME, FATHER?

IN 1756 FRANKLIN WENT TO NEW YORK WITH HIS SON WILLIAM TO LEAVE FOR ENGLAND, BUT THE SAILING WAS DELAYED FOR WEEKS... A WHIM OF LORD LOUDEN.
WE COME TO THE DOCK EVERY DAY. THIS WAITING IS NOT ONLY TIRING, IT'S EXPENSIVE!
I WONDER HOW LONG IT'S GOING TO TAKE LORD LOUDEN TO FINISH THOSE LETTERS HE INSISTS HE MUST FINISH BEFORE WE SAIL?
FINALLY, THEY SAILED...
THOSE OTHER SHIPS ARE BOUND FOR HALIFAX. I WONDER WHY WE STAY WITH THEM SO LONG?
PERHAPS THERE ARE ENEMY SHIPS IN THESE WATERS!
PARDON ME, CAPTAIN, BUT YOU MUST BE CARRYING TOO MUCH CARGO. WE ARE TOO FAR INTO THE WATER. IT'S DANGEROUS TO SAIL THIS WAY!
YOU'RE RIGHT, MR FRANKLIN. I'M HAVING THE CARGO SHIFTED ABOUT. THAT WILL HELP.
A FRENCH PRIVATEER IS CHASING US!
FULL SPEED AHEAD! THEY'LL NEVER CATCH US!
THAT NIGHT...
WE'D BETTER MAKE A RUN FOR PORT. I'VE A FEELING THE ENEMY MAY BE FOLLOWING US!
I'LL STATION ANOTHER WATCH AT THE BOW, SIR.
AYE, CAPTAIN.
WHAT IS THAT BRIGHT LIGHT AHEAD? THE WATCH MUST BE SLEEPING...
A LIGHT-HOUSE!
THE CAPTAIN HAS RETIRED! I MUST DO SOMETHING! WE'LL BE WRECKED!

COME ABOUT! ALL SAILS STANDING!
HE'S TAKING A GREAT RISK IN SO LITTLE SPACE... WE MIGHT CAPSIZE!
THE SHIP STRAINED ABOUT, CHANGING HER COURSE...
I HOPE YOU WILL OVERLOOK MY HASTE IN GIVING ORDERS WITHOUT CONSULTING YOU, CAPTAIN, BUT WE HAD TO ACT FAST.
I'M PROUD OF YOU, SON. WE WOULD BE PILED UP ON THOSE ROCKS, BUT FOR YOUR QUICK THINKING!
WE'RE RUNNING INTO FOG, MR FRANKLIN, BUT WE'LL DOCK WHEN IT LIFTS!
IF WE MUST WAIT, WE MUST. BUT I'LL BE GLAD TO SEE FALMOUTH.
THE NEXT MORNING...
IT'S GOOD TO BE ON LAND AGAIN. WHAT A CROSSING!
IT MUST BE SUNDAY. CHURCH BELLS, HEAR THEM?
LET US GO IN, WILLIAM, AND GIVE THANKS FOR ARRIVING HERE SAFELY.
YOU ARE RIGHT... WE HAVE SURVIVED MANY DANGERS!

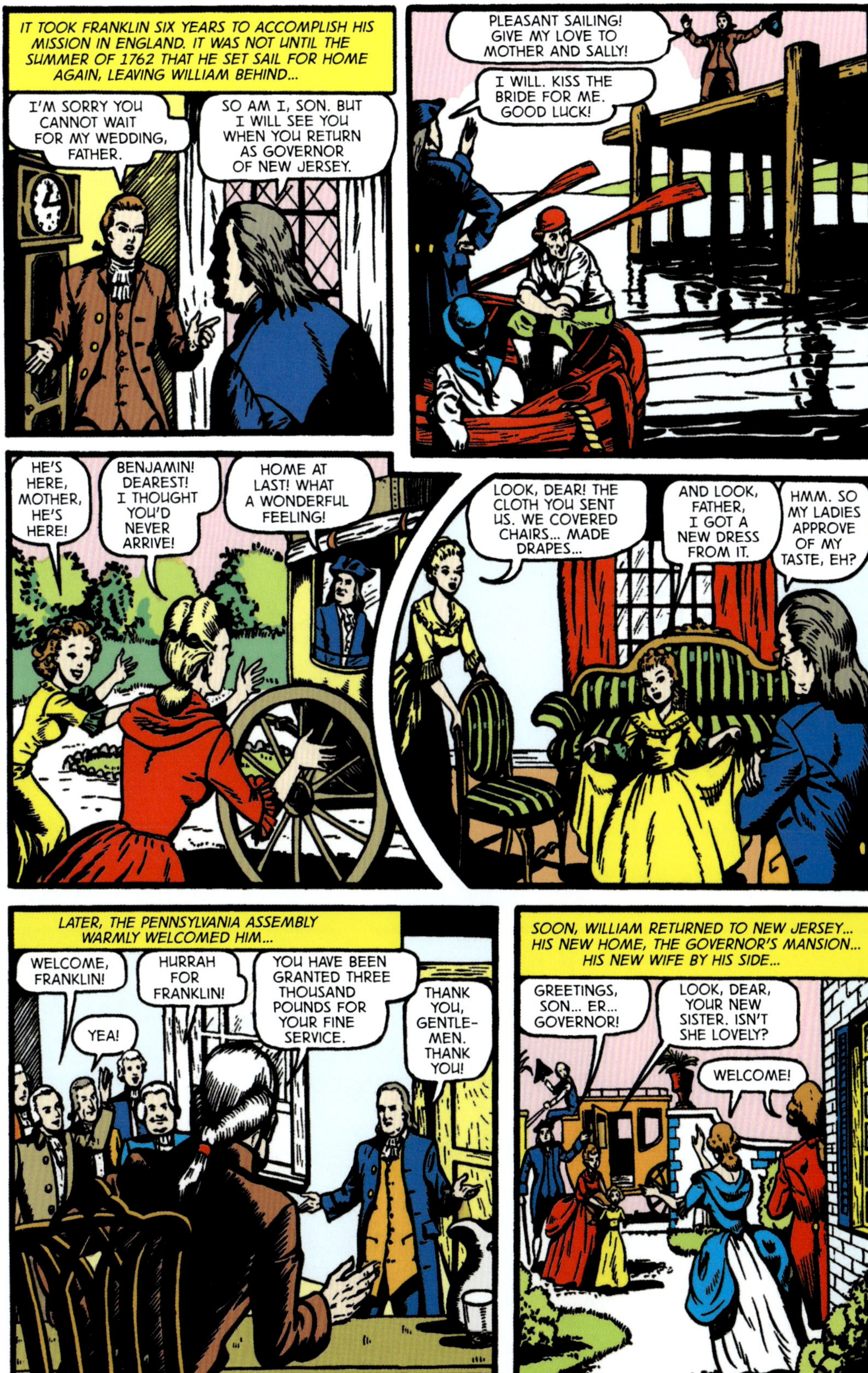
IT TOOK FRANKLIN SIX YEARS TO ACCOMPLISH HIS MISSION IN ENGLAND. IT WAS NOT UNTIL THE SUMMER OF 1762 THAT HE SET SAIL FOR HOME AGAIN, LEAVING WILLIAM BEHIND...
I'M SORRY YOU CANNOT WAIT FOR MY WEDDING, FATHER.
SO AM I, SON. BUT I WILL SEE YOU WHEN YOU RETURN AS GOVERNOR OF NEW JERSEY.
PLEASANT SAILING! GIVE MY LOVE TO MOTHER AND SALLY!
I WILL. KISS THE BRIDE FOR ME. GOOD LUCK!
HE'S HERE, MOTHER, HE'S HERE!
BENJAMIN! DEAREST! I THOUGHT YOU'D NEVER ARRIVE!
HOME AT LAST! WHAT A WONDERFUL FEELING!
LOOK, DEAR! THE CLOTH YOU SENT US. WE COVERED CHAIRS... MADE DRAPES...
AND LOOK, FATHER, I GOT A NEW DRESS FROM IT.
HMM. SO MY LADIES APPROVE OF MY TASTE, EH?
LATER, THE PENNSYLVANIA ASSEMBLY WARMLY WELCOMED HIM...
WELCOME, FRANKLIN!
HURRAH FOR FRANKLIN!
YEA!
YOU HAVE BEEN GRANTED THREE THOUSAND POUNDS FOR YOUR FINE SERVICE.
THANK YOU, GENTLE-MEN. THANK YOU!
SOON, WILLIAM RETURNED TO NEW JERSEY... HIS NEW HOME, THE GOVERNOR'S MANSION... HIS NEW WIFE BY HIS SIDE...
GREETINGS, SON... ER... GOVERNOR!
LOOK, DEAR, YOUR NEW SISTER. ISN'T SHE LOVELY?
WELCOME!

ALTHOUGH THE PEACE OF PARIS HAD BEEN SIGNED BY FRANCE AND ENGLAND, TROUBLE BETWEEN THE COLONIES AND THE INDIANS CONTINUED.
A GROUP OF VILLAGERS CALLED ON THE GOVERNOR OF PENNSYLVANIA.
WE MUST BE PROTECTED FROM THE BARBAROUS REDSKINS.
WHAT CAN I DO? THE STATE HAS NO MONEY TO USE FOR DEFENCE!
IF HE WON'T HELP US, WE'LL HAVE TO HELP OURSELVES!
WE'LL EXTERMINATE THE SAVAGES!
SOME OF THESE PAGANS WON'T BURN ANY MORE HOMES!
KILL THE RED DEVILS!
THE ACTIONS OF THE COLONISTS IS MONSTROUS! TWO WRONGS DON'T MAKE A RIGHT.
THERE'S NOT MUCH ANYONE CAN DO ABOUT IT.
I SPEAK FOR MY PEOPLE. WHITE MAN, HE FOLLOW MY PEOPLE WITH GUN AND HATCHET. WE ASK YOU, SAVE US.
THIS IS SERIOUS!

EVEN GOVERNOR PENN, AT HIS WIT'S END, APPEALED TO FRANKLIN FOR HELP.
SOMETHING MUST BE DONE, FRANKLIN. WHAT DO YOU SUGGEST?
ORGANISE FOR DEFENCE! COLLECT A REGIMENT!
I'LL MAKE MY HEADQUARTERS HERE AT YOUR HOME UNTIL THIS SITUATION CLEARS UP. SEE WHAT YOU CAN DO TO HELP, FRANKLIN!
THE INDIANS ARE QUARTERED IN THE BARRACKS. WE'LL RIDE OUT AND STOP THE WHITE MOB.
THE MOB IS ONLY SEVEN MILES AWAY! THEY'RE HEAVILY ARMED!
THANK YOU, RUNNER. WE'LL RIDE TO MEET THEM!
DIG THE TRENCH ALL AROUND, MY QUAKER FRIENDS. THE CITY IS WELL GUARDED; SEE THAT THE BARRACKS ARE ALSO!
THAT'S WHAT WE MEAN TO DO, MR FRANKLIN. THE INDIANS FEAR FOR THEIR LIVES!
LATER, FRANKLIN MET UP WITH THE ANGRY ADVANCING MOB.
'TWILL DO NO GOOD TO GO ON. THE INDIANS ARE TOO WELL GUARDED FOR YOU TO CAPTURE. TURN BACK!
WE'LL TAKE YOUR ADVICE THIS TIME, BUT NEXT TIME WE'LL GET 'EM!
TROUBLE WAS AVERTED, BUT FRANKLIN GOT NO THANKS FOR HIS TROUBLE...
I'LL POST THIS NOTICE OFFERING REWARDS FOR INDIAN SCALPS, GOVERNOR.
FINE! THAT VILLAIN, FRANKLIN, WILL OBJECT, NO DOUBT!

THE NEXT YEAR, 1764, FRANKLIN RETURNED TO ENGLAND TO BRING ABOUT AN UNDERSTANDING BETWEEN THE ASSEMBLY AND THE GOVERNOR... BUT IN ENGLAND, HIS BUSINESS WAS OVER-SHADOWED BY THE PROPOSED STAMP TAX ON THE COLONIES.
LORD GRANVILLE CALLED THE COLONIAL AGENTS TO HIS CHAMBERS...
THERE'S NOT ENOUGH MONEY FOR SUCH A TAX!
I THINK THE COLONISTS WOULD PREFER THE TAX COLLECTED BY SOME OF THEIR OWN PEOPLE.
THEY WON'T LIKE IT, NO MATTER WHO COLLECTS IT!
THE COLONISTS WILL NEVER STAND FOR IT!
THIS WILL CAUSE TROUBLE!
WHILE IN AMERICA...
WHY SHOULD WE PAY FOR ENGLAND'S WARS?
IT'S ILLEGAL!
NOTICE! BY ORDER OF HIS MAJESTY KING GEORGE THE THIRD.. A TAX WILL BE LEVIED
THAT'S NOT FAIR!
I SHILLING
AT THE PHILADELPHIA WHARF...
HERE COME THE SHIPS WITH THE STAMPS. I HOPE THEY SINK!
THE FLAGS ON OUR SHIPS ARE AT HALF MAST IN PROTEST, BUT THAT'S NOT THE ONLY WAY WE'LL SHOW OUR OBJECTIONS!
SINK! SINK!
NEW HAMPSHIRE DISPLAYED HER SENTIMENTS...
LIBERTY
LIBERTY IS DEAD!
IT WAS KILLED BY STAMPS AND TAXATION!

IN LONDON FRANKLIN ADDRESSED PARLIAMENT FOR THE REPEAL OF THE STAMP ACT...
THE COLONISTS RESENT THIS FORM OF TAXATION. IT IS THE MOTHER OF MISCHIEF!
TIRELESSLY WORKING ON THE REPEAL, HE TESTIFIED IN THE HOUSE OF COMMONS...
WHAT WAS THE TEMPER OF AMERICA TOWARDS GREAT BRITAIN PRIOR TO 1763?
THE BEST IN THE WORLD! NOW IT IS VERY MUCH ALTERED!
RIOTS CONTINUED IN AMERICA... ANGRY CROWDS GATHERED ON NEW YORK STREETS...
BOYCOTT ALL BRITISH GOODS!
YEA! WE'LL DO WITHOUT OR MAKE OUR OWN!
FOUR MONTHS LATER...
AHOY! WE'VE NEWS FROM ENGLAND. THE STAMP ACT HAS BEEN REPEALED!
HURRAY! AT LAST!
AT LAST!
GOD SAVE THE KING!
WE'VE GIFTS FOR THE SAILORS WHO BROUGHT THE GOOD NEWS!
COME AND GET THEM, MATES!

BUT THE COLONISTS' PLEASURE WAS SHORT-LIVED...
BY ORDER OF HIS MAJESTY, YOU WILL HOUSE AND FEED ALL THE KING'S SOLDIERS STATIONED IN NEW YORK.
WHY SHOULD WE?
AT WHOSE EXPENSE?
MORE TAXES! ON TEA, AND PAPER AND GLASS... PAINT... WHAT NEXT?
WE WON'T PAY THEM! WE WEREN'T CONSULTED!
LOOK! THEY'RE SENDING MEN TO COLLECT THE TAXES!
THEY WON'T FORCE US TO PAY, NO MATTER WHAT!
AT BOWLING GREEN, AN EFFIGY OF THE GOVERNOR AND THE PRINCE OF DARKNESS WERE HUNG SIDE BY SIDE ON A MAKESHIFT GALLOWS...
THAT'S WHAT WE THINK OF YOU!
BILL OF LADING
PUSH HIS CARRIAGE INTO THE FIRE WITH HIM!
I HEAR THEY'RE DOING THIS SORT OF THING ALL OVER THE COLONIES!
THAT'S AS IT SHOULD BE! THEY CAN'T FORCE INJUSTICE ON US!

DECEMBER, 1773 FOUND REBELLION RUNNING HIGH IN BOSTON...
AS A MERCHANT, I KNOW THAT THE EAST INDIA COMPANY HAS THE MONOPOLY ON THE TEA TRADE AND THE TAXES ARE TERRIFIC!
WE WON'T BUY IT! WE'LL DO WITHOUT IT!
WE WON'T ACCEPT IT! THEY NEEDN'T BOTHER TO LAND!
WE DEMAND THAT YOU TEA AGENTS RESIGN. TAKE YOUR TEA AND CLEAR OUT OF HERE!
THIS IS REBELLION! THE KING WILL HEAR ABOUT THIS!
TO GET AWAY FROM THE ANGRY MOB, TEA AGENTS SOUGHT REFUGE AT CASTLE WILLIAMS, AN OLD FORT...
THESE COLONISTS ARE GETTING VIOLENT!
WE'LL BE SAFE HERE UNTIL THE MOB BREAKS UP.
THE GOVERNOR WON'T SIGN THE SAILING PERMIT. HE SENT THOSE MEN-OF-WAR TO PROTECT THE TEA SHIPS!
IT WILL DO HIM NO GOOD. WE'LL NOT LET HIM LAND THAT CARGO!
PROTEST MEETINGS FILLED THE PUBLIC SQUARE...
...TAXED WITHOUT HAVING ANY VOICE IN THE MATTER...
ADAMS IS RIGHT! IT'S TIME WE TOOK ACTION!

THUS THE PEOPLE OF BOSTON TOOK MATTERS INTO THEIR OWN HANDS...
WE MUST DO SOMETHING TO PROVE ONCE AND FOR ALL THAT WE'LL NOT PAY THESE OUTRAGEOUS TAXES. NOW I HAVE AN IDEA...
LET'S HEAR IT, FRIEND!
SO LATER THAT NIGHT, ON THE WHARF...
I WONDER WHAT'S KEEPING THEM? WE'VE GOT TO ACT SWIFTLY!
YES, THE BRITISH MUST NOT SUSPECT.
WE THOUGHT YOU'D NEVER GET HERE! DO A GOOD JOB NOW!
HAVE NO FEAR. THAT TEA WILL BE WELL FLAVOURED WITH SALT WHEN WE GET THROUGH WITH IT!
ALL SEEMS TO BE QUIET WITH THE BRITISH.
WE'VE GOT TO TAKE CARE TO KEEP IT SO!
SHHH! WE'LL TAKE THEM BY SURPRISE!
AND IT WILL BE THE SURPRISE OF THEIR LIVES!

WITH THE STEALTH OF INDIANS, THE MEN BOARDED ONE OF THE BRITISH SHIPS...
BE PREPARED! ANYTHING CAN HAPPEN!
PEACEFUL AS BABIES! IT'S PLAIN TO SEE THAT THEY WEREN'T EXPECTING COMPANY!
INDIANS! RUN FOR YOUR LIVES, MATES! THEY'LL SCALP YE!
AYE! BUT WE DO IT WITH OUR FISTS!
NICE AND TIDY NOW, CHIEF TWO FEATHERS. WE DON'T WANT TO HURT THE NICE MAN.
YOU'RE NOT REAL INDIANS!
AREN'T WE NOW?
THEY'LL NEVER COLLECT TAXES ON THIS PRECIOUS CARGO. NOT UNLESS THEY'RE DEEP SEA DIVERS!
OVER IT GOES!
TEA
THUS, A GLOWING PAGE IN AMERICAN HISTORY WAS WRITTEN... THE BOSTON TEA PARTY!

FRANKLIN'S RETURN TO AMERICA FOUND MANY PAINFUL CHANGES... DEATH HAD VISITED HIS BELOVED WIFE, AND THE FIRST BATTLES OF THE REVOLUTION HAD BEEN FOUGHT...
IF MOTHER WERE ONLY HERE TO GREET HIM... HE'LL GRIEVE SORELY FOR HER...
HE STILL HAS US, SALLY.
AH! MY DAUGHTER AND HER HUSBAND. AND THOSE MUST BE MY NEW GRANDCHILDREN.
THAT NIGHT AT FRANKLIN'S HOME, HE LISTENED TO A GRIM ACCOUNT OF THE WAR...
AYE. THE BATTLES OF CONCORD AND LEXINGTON WERE BLOODY BUSINESS...
"PAUL REVERE RODE TO WARN THE PATRIOTS...
THE BRITISH COME! TO LEXINGTON AT ONCE!
DEPEND ON US. WE'LL BE THERE!
"WHILE AT LEXINGTON, THE PATRIOTS GATHERED EN MASSE, CRUDELY ARMED... EVEN WITH THEIR FARM IMPLEMENTS...
WE'LL STOP THEM!
IT'S ABOUT TIME THEY KNEW WE MEAN BUSINESS!
"FINALLY, THE BRITISH ARRIVED...
TAKE HEED, REBELS, DISPERSE! LAY DOWN YOUR ARMS OR WE'LL ATTACK!
"A SINGLE REPLY RANG OUT...
NEVER!
"VASTLY OUTNUMBERED AND PITIFULLY UNDERARMED, THE VALIANT MEN WERE SOON ROUTED BY BRITISH MUSKETS..."
FIRE AND FIRE AGAIN TILL THERE'S NOT A REBEL STANDING!

"UNDAUNTED, THE PATRIOTS RE-GATHERED AT CONCORD...
THE BRITISH ARE COMING!
THIS TIME WE'LL STOP THEM. WE'RE BETTER ARMED NOW.
FIX BY THE BRIDGE!
"AND AGAIN THE TWO SIDES CLASHED..."
WE'RE OVER-POWERING THEM!
KEEP A STEADY STREAM OF FIRE, MEN. THAT'LL DO IT!
WHAT SHALL WE DO, SIR?
I FEAR FOR THE WORST. THEY WAR LIKE SAVAGES. NO ORDER!
RETREAT! RUN FOR YOUR LIVES!
...AND SO THE BRITISH WERE FORCED BACK TO BOSTON.
IT IS SAD INDEED THAT DISPUTES OF COUNTRIES MUST BE SETTLED WITH MEN'S BLOOD!

TAKING IMMEDIATE ACTION, FRANKLIN JOINED THE FIRST CONTINENTAL CONGRESS... HE CONFERRED WITH GEORGE WASHINGTON AND THOMAS JEFFERSON...
BUT I FEEL THAT A PETITION TO THE KING WOULD BE USELESS, MR WASHINGTON.
YET WE MUST UTILISE EVERY MEANS AT OUR COMMAND TO AVERT THIS CONFLICT.
AT HOME, THERE WAS THE MATTER OF PRINCIPLE...
BUT FATHER, YOU'VE BEEN A MEMBER OF THE ASSEMBLY FOR SO MANY YEARS!
I KNOW, BUT THEY DEMAND AN OATH OF ALLEGIANCE TO THE KING. I REFUSE TO TAKE IT, SALLY.
YET FRANKLIN'S SON, WILLIAM, WAS A STAUNCH LOYALIST... HIS FATHER'S ATTITUDE DIFFERED FROM HIS.
WELL, I'LL REMAIN LOYAL TO MY KING, FATHER. I'M NOT WITH THE REBELS!
I CAN'T AGREE WITH YOU, SON, AND I DO HOPE YOUR OPINION DOESN'T GET YOU INTO TROUBLE!
A FINAL BREAK WITH ENGLAND CAME IN 1775... AT BREED'S HILL*...
HERE THEY COME UP THE HILL, MEN. AIM LOW AND DO NOT FIRE TILL YOU SEE THE WHITES OF THEIR EYES!
LET 'EM COME, GENERAL PUTNAM!
WE'RE READY FOR THEM!
*NEAR THE VILLAGE OF BUNKER HILL, OUTSIDE OF BOSTON, MASS.
IT WAS IMPOSSIBLE FOR THE BRITISH TO ADVANCE... AT FIRST...
...BUT, WILLING TO SUFFER UNBELIEVABLE CASUALTIES, THEY NOT ONLY SUCCEEDED BUT FORCED THE PATRIOTS TO RETREAT.
DEATH TO THE REBELS AT ANY COST!

REALISING THE GREAT LACK OF EQUIPMENT BY THE PATRIOTS, FRANKLIN DESIGNED A NEW WEAPON. A PIKE TO TAKE THE PLACE OF THE LACKING BAYONETS...
OUR MEN ARE BRILLIANT MARKSMEN, BUT BUNKER HILL TAUGHT US THE NEED OF THIS.
WE'LL HAVE THEM MADE AT ONCE, BEN!
THE MOUTH OF THE DELAWARE ALSO RECEIVED A NEW DEFENCE...
THESE CONTRAPTIONS WILL SINK AND KEEP THE BRITISH WAR VESSELS WITHIN RANGE OF THE TOWN.
WE MUST KEEP THEIR LOCATION A SECRET ENTRUSTED ONLY TO THESE HONEST PILOTS!
HEAVE HO, MEN!
AND AT THE PHILADELPHIA WHARF, A TWELVE-OARED, TWO-GUNNED BOAT FORMIDABLY APPEARED...
THESE ROW-GALLEYS ARE FLOATING FORTS!
THIS SHOULD BE AN UNPLEASANT SURPRISE TO THE ENEMY!
AGAIN THE COMMITTEE MET...
WE'RE RUNNING LOW ON POWDER AND LEAD, GENTLEMEN, BUT THERE'S STILL A WAR TO WIN. I SUGGEST USING BOWS AND ARROWS.
THAT'S A POOR MATCH FOR BRITISH SHELLS!
NAVAL OFFICERS WERE CHOSEN TO COMMAND THE ARMED BOATS...
GOOD LUCK, MEN. YOU HAVE BEEN CHOSEN FOR TRUSTWORTHINESS AS WELL AS ABILITY. WE EXPECT A GREAT DEAL FROM THESE BOATS.
WE WON'T LET YOU DOWN, SIR!
MEDICINE AND OTHER SUPPLIES WERE PREPARED IN ADVANCE FOR THE TROOPS...
IT IS UP TO YOU TO SEE THAT THESE WAGONS REACH THEIR DESTINATION, DRIVER. I DON'T HAVE TO REMIND YOU OF THEIR IMPORTANCE!
NOTHING WILL DELAY ME, SIR!

IN JUNE, 1776, A COMMITTEE OF FIVE GATHERED IN PHILADELPHIA. THOMAS JEFFERSON, ROGER SHERMAN, ROBERT R LIVINGSTON, JOHN ADAMS AND BENJAMIN FRANKLIN...
I DO NOT FEEL EQUAL TO THE TASK OF WRITING THIS DOCUMENT, MR ADAMS. BUT I'M SURE MR JEFFERSON COULD DO IT MORE EFFECTIVELY AND WITH ELOQUENCE.
YES, I TOO BELIEVE HE COULD PRODUCE A STIRRING DOCUMENT!
IN CONGRESS, JULY 4, 1776.
THUS, FROM THE STATE HOUSE STEPS ON THAT MEMORABLE DAY, JULY 8TH, 1776, THE DECLARATION OF INDEPENDENCE WAS READ TO AN ENTHUSIASTIC, CHEERING CROWD AND A SPARK FROM THE TORCH OF LIBERTY BURNED IN EACH MAN'S HEART.
...AMONG THESE ARE LIFE, LIBERTY AND THE PURSUIT OF HAPPINESS...
YEA!
HEAR! HEAR!
AND THE LIBERTY BELL RANG OUT...
PROCLAIM LIBERTY
INHABITANTS THERE
HERE'S MY SIGNATURE, MR FRANKLIN. I HOPE I WRITE SO THAT GEORGE THE THIRD MAY READ WITHOUT HIS SPECTACLES.
WE MUST ALL HANG TOGETHER, OR MOST ASSUREDLY WE WILL ALL HANG SEPARATELY, MR HANCOCK!

FRANCE, EAGER TO DISCREDIT HER OLD ENEMY, ENGLAND, UNOFFICIALLY HELPED THE COLONIES... SECRET AGENTS ARTHUR LEE AND BARON DE BEAUMARCHAIS CONFERRED IN LONDON...
HOW CAN WE DO THIS SECRETLY, BARON?
LEAVE THAT TO ME.
I HAVE SPOKEN TO THE BRITISH MINISTERS... THEY KNOW WHAT THEY'RE IN FOR, BUT THE AMERICANS NEED SUPPLIES!
I THINK I CAN GET YOU HELP, LEE, BUT NO ONE MUST KNOW THE FRENCH GOVERNMENT IS INVOLVED...
A FICTITIOUS "RODERIGUE HORTALEZ AND COMPANY" WAS SET UP...
WE WILL OPERATE THIS LIKE A REGULAR BUSINESS CONCERN!
NO ONE NEED KNOW THAT VERGENNES HAS PROMISED TO ADVANCE A MILLION FRANCS FOR AMMUNITION AND CLOTHING FOR AMERICAN SOLDIERS!
LATER, AT A PORT IN MARTINIQUE, AGENTS HERALDED THE ARRIVAL OF AMERICAN SHIPS...
HERE THEY COME AT LAST! THREE OF THEM GOT THROUGH ALL RIGHT!
GOODS WERE RESHIPPED TO AMERICA...
THE AMMUNITION AND CLOTHING ARE SORELY NEEDED BY OUR TROOPS!
LET US HOPE THAT IT REACHES THEM SAFELY...
FRENCH NAVAL SQUADRONS PROTECTED THE SHIPPING...
I SEE NOTHING!
THESE ENGLISH... WE FRIGHTEN THEM...

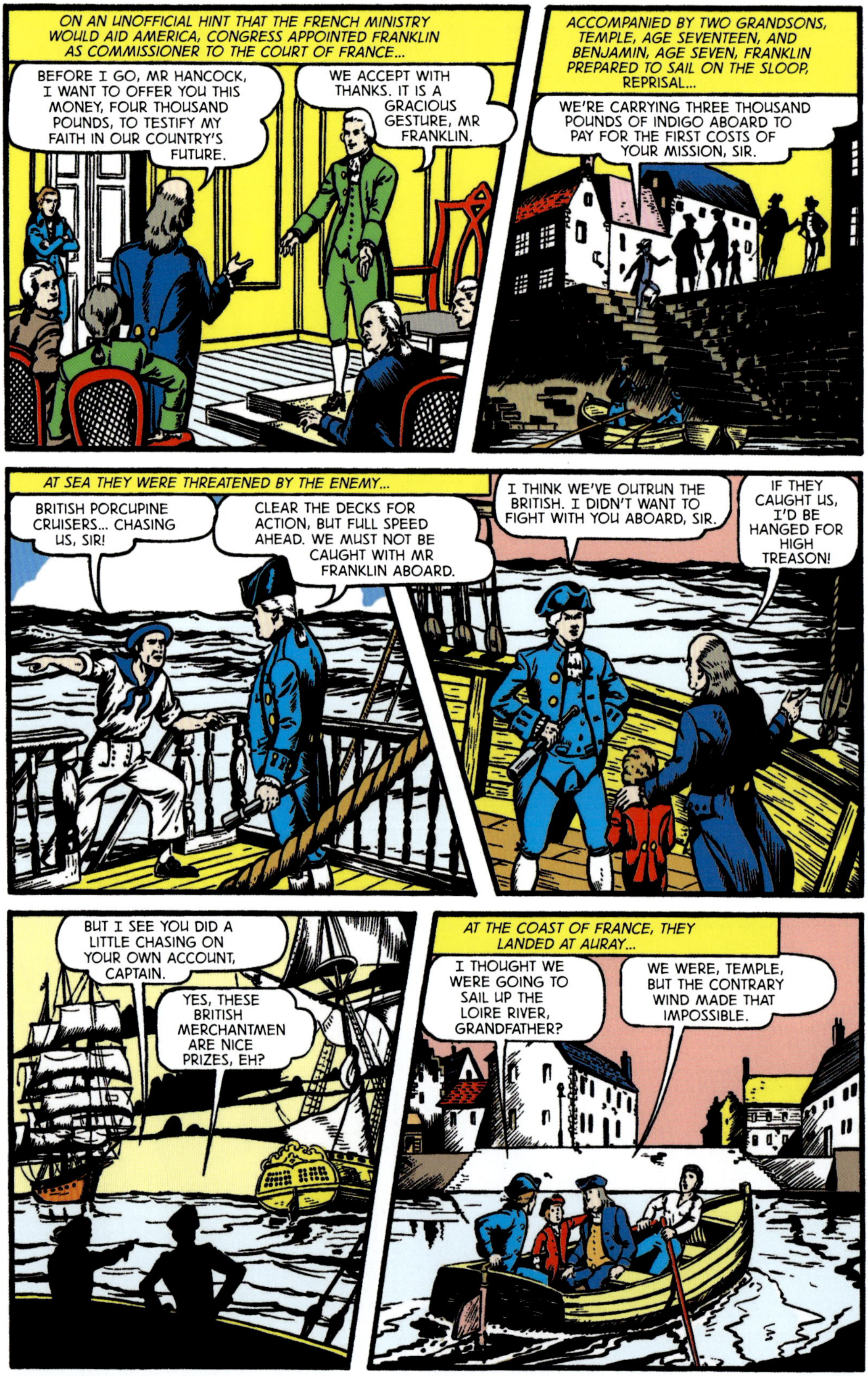
ON AN UNOFFICIAL HINT THAT THE FRENCH MINISTRY WOULD AID AMERICA, CONGRESS APPOINTED FRANKLIN AS COMMISSIONER TO THE COURT OF FRANCE...
BEFORE I GO, MR HANCOCK, I WANT TO OFFER YOU THIS MONEY, FOUR THOUSAND POUNDS, TO TESTIFY MY FAITH IN OUR COUNTRY'S FUTURE.
WE ACCEPT WITH THANKS. IT IS A GRACIOUS GESTURE, MR FRANKLIN.
ACCOMPANIED BY TWO GRANDSONS, TEMPLE, AGE SEVENTEEN, AND BENJAMIN, AGE SEVEN, FRANKLIN PREPARED TO SAIL ON THE SLOOP, REPRISAL...
WE'RE CARRYING THREE THOUSAND POUNDS OF INDIGO ABOARD TO PAY FOR THE FIRST COSTS OF YOUR MISSION, SIR.
AT SEA THEY WERE THREATENED BY THE ENEMY...
BRITISH PORCUPINE CRUISERS... CHASING US, SIR!
CLEAR THE DECKS FOR ACTION, BUT FULL SPEED AHEAD. WE MUST NOT BE CAUGHT WITH MR FRANKLIN ABOARD.
I THINK WE'VE OUTRUN THE BRITISH. I DIDN'T WANT TO FIGHT WITH YOU ABOARD, SIR.
IF THEY CAUGHT US, I'D BE HANGED FOR HIGH TREASON!
BUT I SEE YOU DID A LITTLE CHASING ON YOUR OWN ACCOUNT, CAPTAIN.
YES, THESE BRITISH MERCHANTMEN ARE NICE PRIZES, EH?
AT THE COAST OF FRANCE, THEY LANDED AT AURAY...
I THOUGHT WE WERE GOING TO SAIL UP THE LOIRE RIVER, GRANDFATHER?
WE WERE, TEMPLE, BUT THE CONTRARY WIND MADE THAT IMPOSSIBLE.

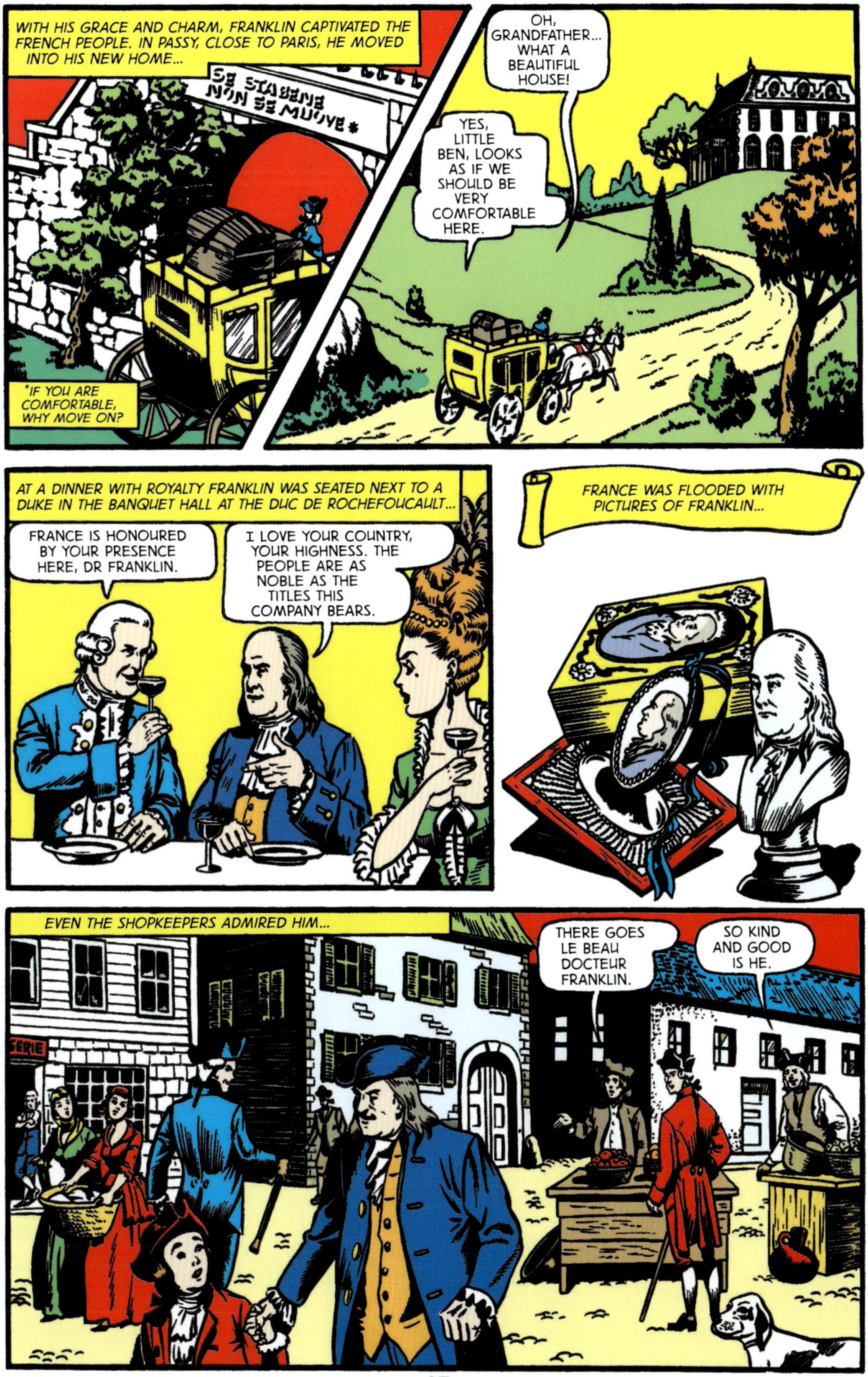

WITH HIS GRACE AND CHARM, FRANKLIN CAPTIVATED THE FRENCH PEOPLE. IN PASSY, CLOSE TO PARIS, HE MOVED INTO HIS NEW HOME...
SE STABENE NON SE MUOVE *
*IF YOU ARE COMFORTABLE, WHY MOVE ON?
OH, GRANDFATHER... WHAT A BEAUTIFUL HOUSE!
YES, LITTLE BEN, LOOKS AS IF WE SHOULD BE VERY COMFORTABLE HERE.
AT A DINNER WITH ROYALTY FRANKLIN WAS SEATED NEXT TO A DUKE IN THE BANQUET HALL AT THE DUC DE ROCHEFOUCAULT...
FRANCE IS HONOURED BY YOUR PRESENCE HERE, DR FRANKLIN.
I LOVE YOUR COUNTRY, YOUR HIGHNESS. THE PEOPLE ARE AS NOBLE AS THE TITLES THIS COMPANY BEARS.
FRANCE WAS FLOODED WITH PICTURES OF FRANKLIN...
EVEN THE SHOPKEEPERS ADMIRED HIM...
THERE GOES LE BEAU DOCTEUR FRANKLIN.
SO KIND AND GOOD IS HE.

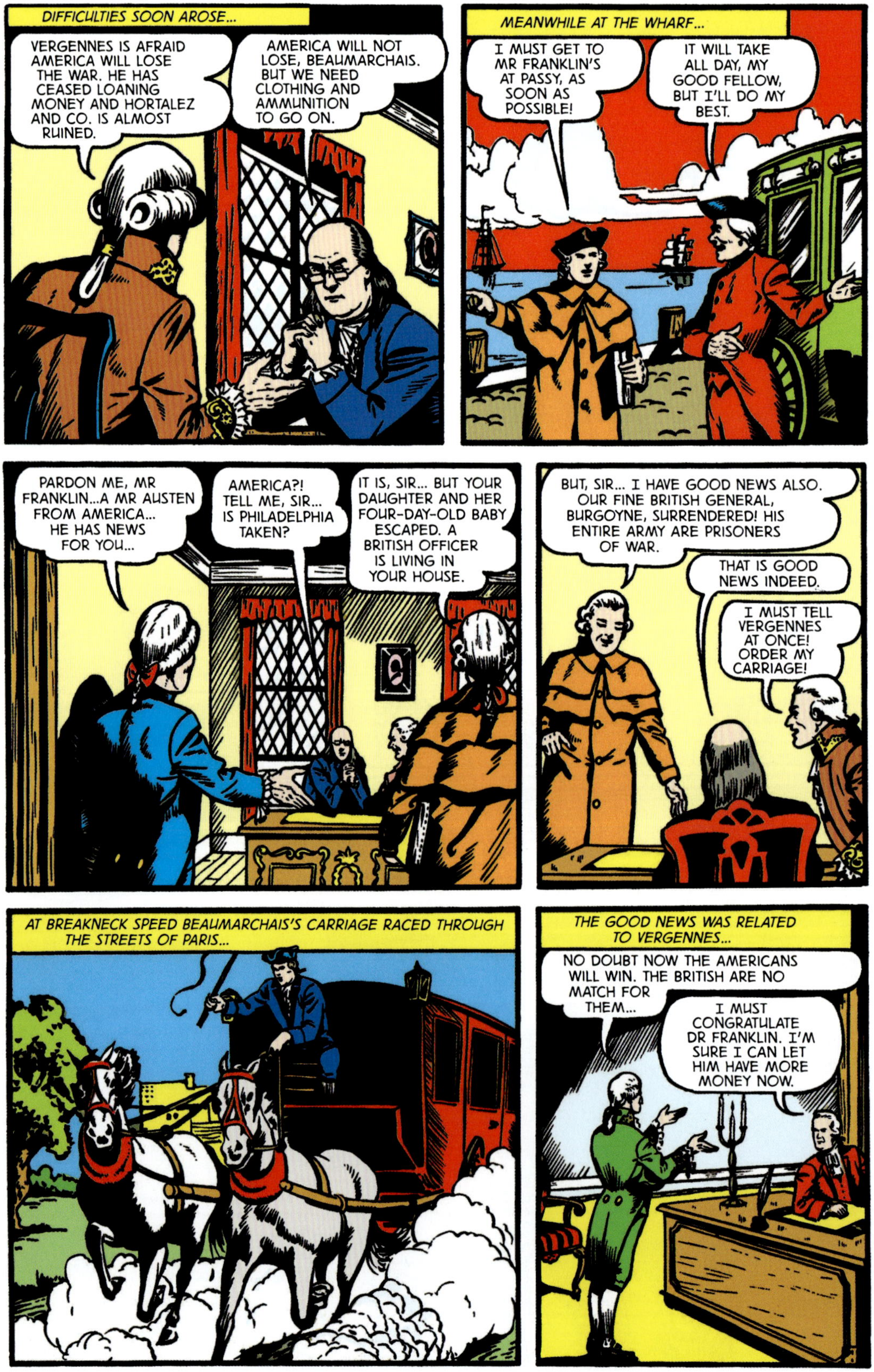
DIFFICULTIES SOON AROSE...
VERGENNES IS AFRAID AMERICA WILL LOSE THE WAR. HE HAS CEASED LOANING MONEY AND HORTALEZ AND CO. IS ALMOST RUINED.
AMERICA WILL NOT LOSE, BEAUMARCHAIS. BUT WE NEED CLOTHING AND AMMUNITION TO GO ON.
MEANWHILE AT THE WHARF...
I MUST GET TO MR FRANKLIN'S AT PASSY, AS SOON AS POSSIBLE!
IT WILL TAKE ALL DAY, MY GOOD FELLOW, BUT I'LL DO MY BEST.
PARDON ME, MR FRANKLIN...A MR AUSTEN FROM AMERICA... HE HAS NEWS FOR YOU...
AMERICA?! TELL ME, SIR... IS PHILADELPHIA TAKEN?
IT IS, SIR... BUT YOUR DAUGHTER AND HER FOUR-DAY-OLD BABY ESCAPED. A BRITISH OFFICER IS LIVING IN YOUR HOUSE.
BUT, SIR... I HAVE GOOD NEWS ALSO. OUR FINE BRITISH GENERAL, BURGOYNE, SURRENDERED! HIS ENTIRE ARMY ARE PRISONERS OF WAR.
THAT IS GOOD NEWS INDEED.
I MUST TELL VERGENNES AT ONCE! ORDER MY CARRIAGE!
AT BREAKNECK SPEED BEAUMARCHAIS'S CARRIAGE RACED THROUGH THE STREETS OF PARIS...
THE GOOD NEWS WAS RELATED TO VERGENNES...
NO DOUBT NOW THE AMERICANS WILL WIN. THE BRITISH ARE NO MATCH FOR THEM...
I MUST CONGRATULATE DR FRANKLIN. I'M SURE I CAN LET HIM HAVE MORE MONEY NOW.

A TREATY OF ALLIANCE BETWEEN AMERICA AND FRANCE WAS PLANNED...
THE COMTE DE VERGENNES CONGRATULATES THE AMERICAN VICTORY. HE WOULD WELCOME YOUR PROPOSAL FOR AN ALLIANCE.
BE SURE, TEMPLE, THAT ONLY VERGENNES HIMSELF RECEIVES THESE PAPERS.
REST ASSURED THAT I WILL. I KNOW HOW SECRET THEY ARE, SIR.
LATER...
HERE COMES VERGENNES'S CARRIAGE FOR US, GENTLEMEN. I WONDER WHERE WE GO FROM HERE?
HE CERTAINLY IS TAKING CARE THAT NO SPIES LEARN OF THE TREATY.
THE CARRIAGE HEADED FOR A SECLUDED HOUSE NEAR VERSAILLES AND THE THREE AMERICANS, FRANKLIN, LEE AND DEANE WONDERED WHAT AWAITED THEM...
A TREATY WAS AGREED UPON... BUT...
WE CANNOT SIGN THIS TREATY UNTIL WE HEAR FROM SPAIN. YET I CAN ASSURE YOU OF FRANCE'S FULL COOPERATION.
YOU ARE RIGHT ABOUT SPAIN, COUNT.
KING LOUIS XVI RECOGNISED THE TREATY BY INVITING FRANKLIN AND HIS PARTY TO A COURT AFFAIR...
HIS MAJESTY REQUESTS YOUR PRESENCE IN COURT, MARCH TWENTIETH, DOCTOR FRANKLIN.
WE ACCEPT WITH PLEASURE.

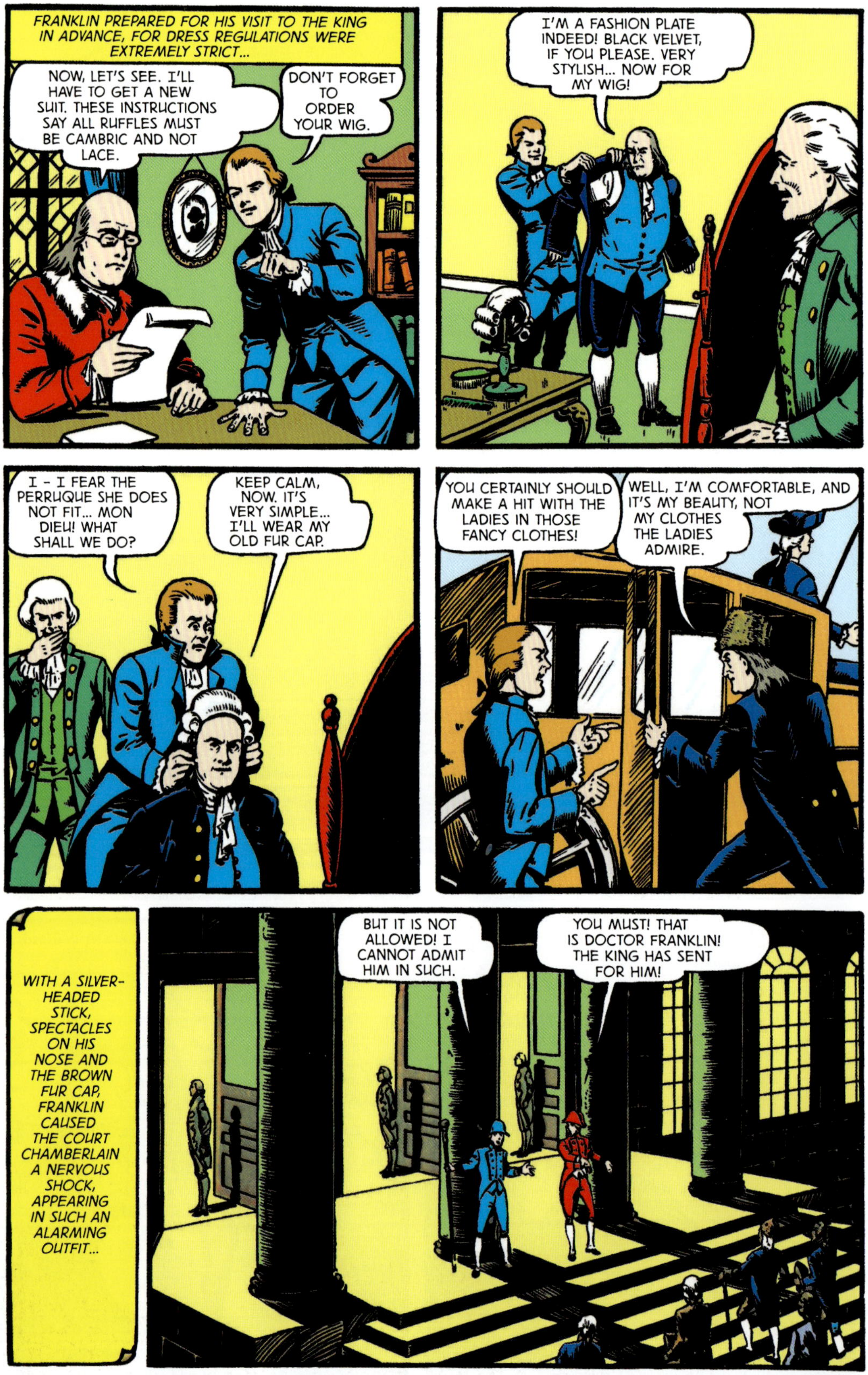
FRANKLIN PREPARED FOR HIS VISIT TO THE KING IN ADVANCE, FOR DRESS REGULATIONS WERE EXTREMELY STRICT...
NOW, LET'S SEE. I'LL HAVE TO GET A NEW SUIT. THESE INSTRUCTIONS SAY ALL RUFFLES MUST BE CAMBRIC AND NOT LACE.
DON'T FORGET TO ORDER YOUR WIG.
I'M A FASHION PLATE INDEED! BLACK VELVET, IF YOU PLEASE. VERY STYLISH... NOW FOR MY WIG!
I - I FEAR THE PERRUQUE SHE DOES NOT FIT... MON DIEU! WHAT SHALL WE DO?
KEEP CALM, NOW. IT'S VERY SIMPLE... I'LL WEAR MY OLD FUR CAP.
YOU CERTAINLY SHOULD MAKE A HIT WITH THE LADIES IN THOSE FANCY CLOTHES!
WELL, I'M COMFORTABLE, AND IT'S MY BEAUTY, NOT MY CLOTHES THE LADIES ADMIRE.
WITH A SILVER-HEADED STICK, SPECTACLES ON HIS NOSE AND THE BROWN FUR CAP, FRANKLIN CAUSED THE COURT CHAMBERLAIN A NERVOUS SHOCK, APPEARING IN SUCH AN ALARMING OUTFIT...
BUT IT IS NOT ALLOWED! I CANNOT ADMIT HIM IN SUCH.
YOU MUST! THAT IS DOCTOR FRANKLIN! THE KING HAS SENT FOR HIM!

THE COURT OF VERSAILLES...
WE WELCOME YOU AND YOUR FRIENDS, DOCTOR FRANKLIN, IN THE NAME OF THE KING AND OF FRANCE.
THIS IS A GREAT AND MEMORABLE HONOUR.
IN THE KING'S DRESSING ROOM, THE AUDIENCE WITH HIS MAJESTY WAS INFORMAL...
ASSURE CONGRESS OF MY FRIENDSHIP. I'M CERTAIN THIS TREATY WILL BE FOR THE GOOD OF OUR TWO NATIONS.
YOUR HIGHNESS MAY COUNT ON THE GRATITUDE OF CONGRESS.
THERE IS DOCTOR FRANKLIN!
THE FOLLOWING DAY...
VIVE L' AMERIQUE!
YEA!
FRANKLIN!
THE KING SEEMED IMPRESSED WITH YOUR CHARM, JUST LIKE THE REST OF US!
IF YOU WOULD REAP PRAISE, YOU MUST SOW THE SEEDS; GENTLE WORDS AND USEFUL DEEDS.

DAYS LATER, IN HIS LIBRARY AT PASSY, FRANKLIN REJOICED AT THE NEWS OF JOHN PAUL JONES'S VICTORY AT SEA...
THAT MUST HAVE BEEN A TERRIFIC BATTLE! WHAT HAPPENED, GRANDFATHER?
ACCORDING TO THIS DISPATCH...
"OFF THE COAST OF SCOTLAND, THE ENEMY WAS SIGHTED.
HERE THEY COME. PREPARE FOR BATTLE! CROWD THE SAIL!
AYE, CAPT'N JONES! YOUR ORDERS WILL BE OBEYED FORTHWITH!
THE ALLIANCE HAS DESERTED US, SIR!
WE'LL MANAGE WITHOUT HER. I DON'T TRUST THAT FRENCH COMMODORE.
"JONES'S FLAGSHIP, AND THE BRITISH SERAPIS ENGAGED IN A BLOODY CONFLICT...
FIRE DIRECTLY AT THEIR MAINMAST... THAT WILL SETTLE THEM!
"BUT SOON THE SERAPIS WAS VANQUISHED!"
THE BRITISH HAVE HAULED DOWN THEIR ENSIGN, SIR!
SIGNAL THAT WE DEMAND COMPLETE SURRENDER!

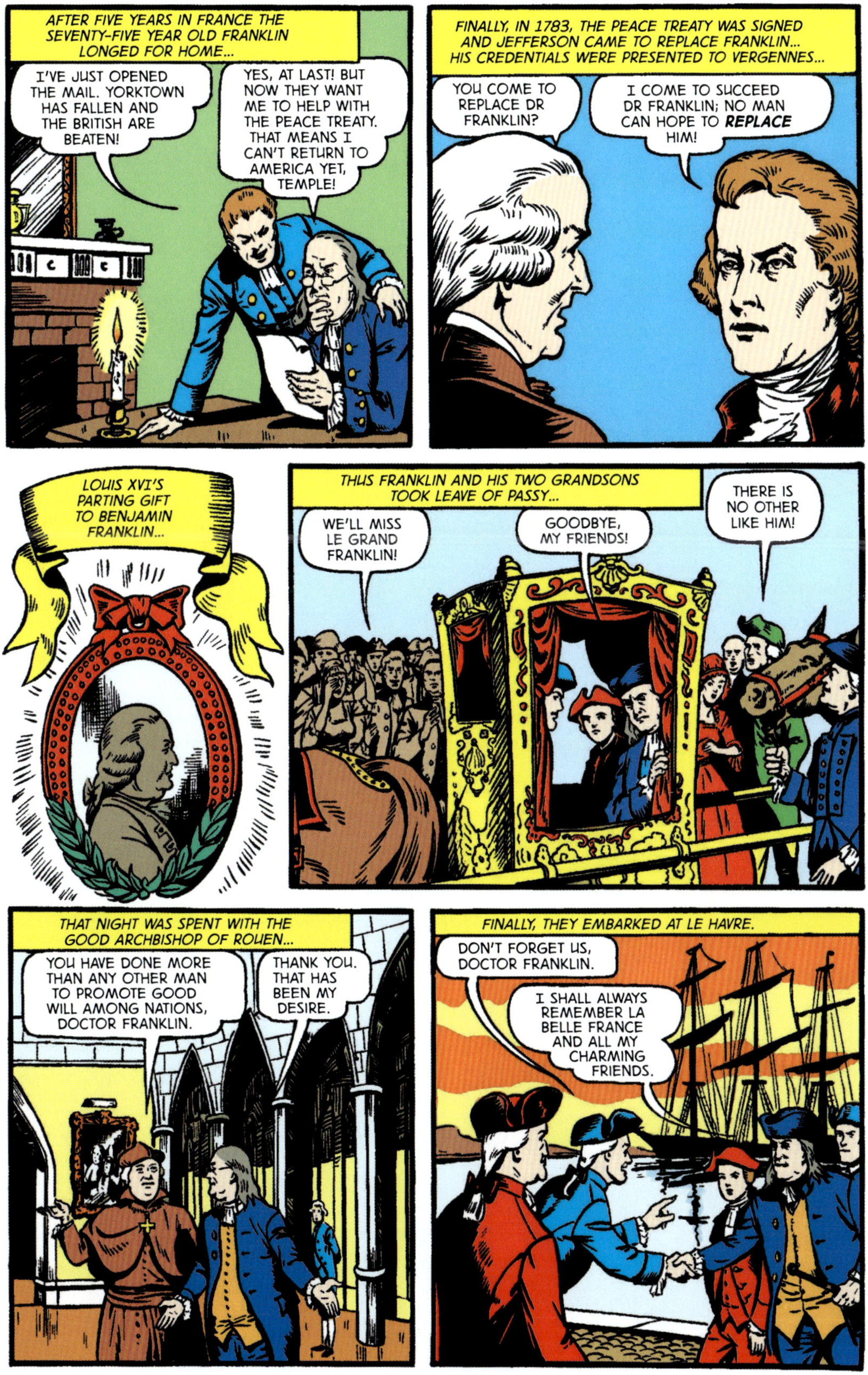
AFTER FIVE YEARS IN FRANCE THE SEVENTY-FIVE YEAR OLD FRANKLIN LONGED FOR HOME...
I'VE JUST OPENED THE MAIL. YORKTOWN HAS FALLEN AND THE BRITISH ARE BEATEN!
YES, AT LAST! BUT NOW THEY WANT ME TO HELP WITH THE PEACE TREATY. THAT MEANS I CAN'T RETURN TO AMERICA YET, TEMPLE!
FINALLY, IN 1783, THE PEACE TREATY WAS SIGNED AND JEFFERSON CAME TO REPLACE FRANKLIN... HIS CREDENTIALS WERE PRESENTED TO VERGENNES...
YOU COME TO REPLACE DR FRANKLIN?
I COME TO SUCCEED DR FRANKLIN; NO MAN CAN HOPE TO **REPLACE** HIM!
LOUIS XVI'S PARTING GIFT TO BENJAMIN FRANKLIN...
THUS FRANKLIN AND HIS TWO GRANDSONS TOOK LEAVE OF PASSY...
WE'LL MISS LE GRAND FRANKLIN!
GOODBYE, MY FRIENDS!
THERE IS NO OTHER LIKE HIM!
THAT NIGHT WAS SPENT WITH THE GOOD ARCHBISHOP OF ROUEN...
YOU HAVE DONE MORE THAN ANY OTHER MAN TO PROMOTE GOOD WILL AMONG NATIONS, DOCTOR FRANKLIN.
THANK YOU. THAT HAS BEEN MY DESIRE.
FINALLY, THEY EMBARKED AT LE HAVRE.
DON'T FORGET US, DOCTOR FRANKLIN.
I SHALL ALWAYS REMEMBER LA BELLE FRANCE AND ALL MY CHARMING FRIENDS.

NOW EIGHTY YEARS OLD, FRANKLIN ARRIVED IN HIS NATIVE LAND AFTER AN ABSENCE OF NINE YEARS...
BUT HIS PUBLIC LIFE WAS HARDLY OVER...
OF THE SEVENTY-SEVEN VOTES, DR FRANKLIN HAS RECEIVED SEVENTY-SIX! HE IS PRESIDENT OF PENNSYLVANIA FOR THE THIRD TIME!
IN 1787 HE RENDERED HIS COUNTRY HIS LAST GREAT SERVICE... THE CONSTITUTIONAL CONVENTION...
IF WE GIVE CONGRESS TOO MUCH POWER, WE SHALL CEASE TO BE A REPUBLIC!
WHEW! THEIR TEMPERS ARE AS HOT AS THE WEATHER.
THE CONSTITUTION ADOPTED... PHILADELPHIA HAD A GREAT CELEBRATION...
THOSE MUST BE THE RHYMES YOU WROTE GRANDFATHER!
PERHAPS! AH, SEEING THAT PRESS TAKES ME BACK TO MY YOUTH...
HIS PUBLIC SERVICE OVER, SICK IN BODY, YET YOUNG IN SPIRIT, FRANKLIN RETIRED TO HIS HOME...
IT IS KIND OF YOU, GENTLEMEN, TO BRING ME THE NEWS OF THE DAY.
AGE DIDN'T DULL FRANKLIN'S INVENTIVE MIND...
YOU SEE, MY CHAIR SERVES TWO PURPOSES... IT'S BOTH A SEAT AND A LADDER.
INGENIOUS CONTRAPTION!

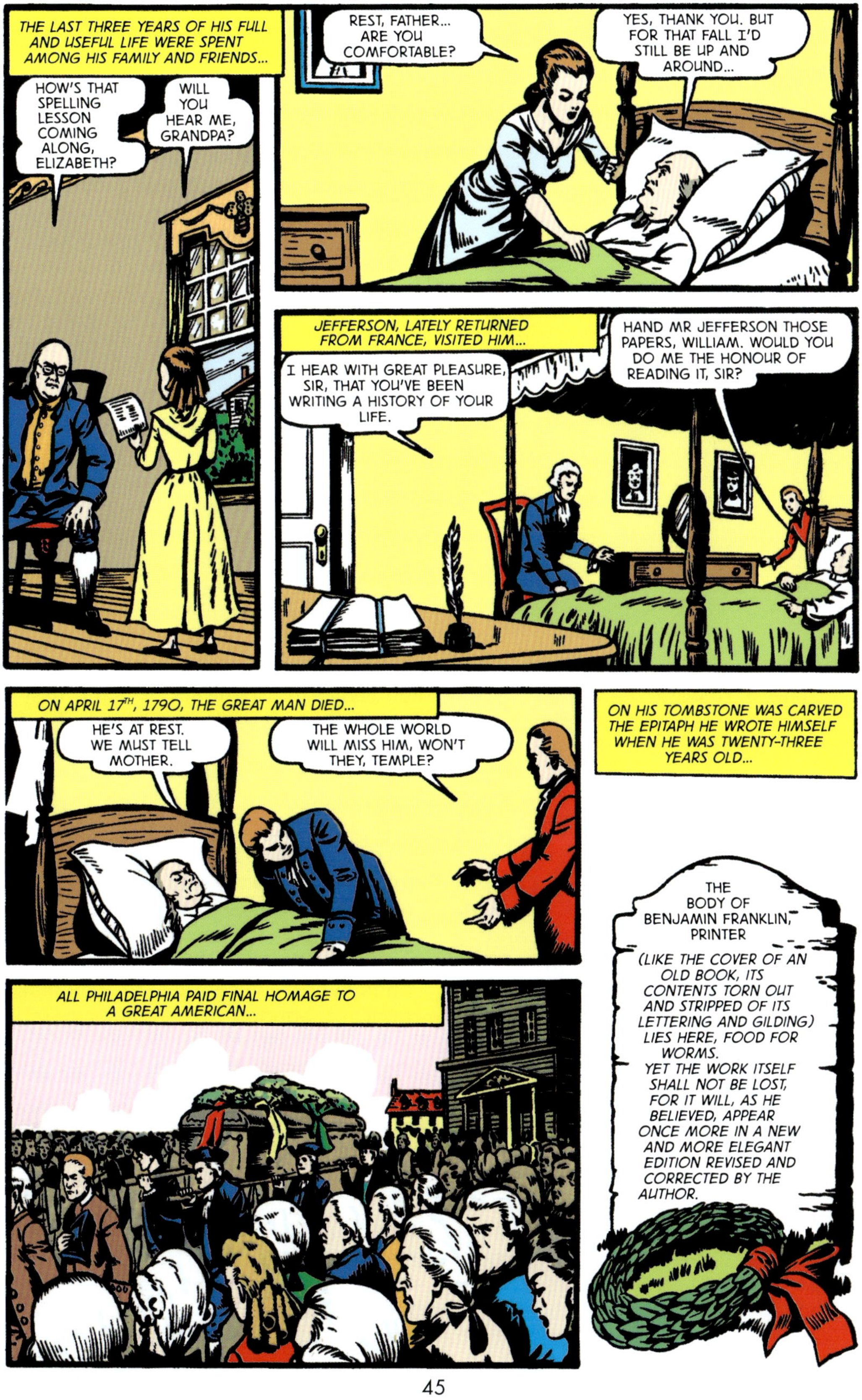
THE LAST THREE YEARS OF HIS FULL AND USEFUL LIFE WERE SPENT AMONG HIS FAMILY AND FRIENDS...
HOW'S THAT SPELLING LESSON COMING ALONG, ELIZABETH?
WILL YOU HEAR ME, GRANDPA?
REST, FATHER... ARE YOU COMFORTABLE?
YES, THANK YOU. BUT FOR THAT FALL I'D STILL BE UP AND AROUND...
JEFFERSON, LATELY RETURNED FROM FRANCE, VISITED HIM...
I HEAR WITH GREAT PLEASURE, SIR, THAT YOU'VE BEEN WRITING A HISTORY OF YOUR LIFE.
HAND MR JEFFERSON THOSE PAPERS, WILLIAM. WOULD YOU DO ME THE HONOUR OF READING IT, SIR?
ON APRIL 17TH, 1790, THE GREAT MAN DIED...
HE'S AT REST. WE MUST TELL MOTHER.
THE WHOLE WORLD WILL MISS HIM, WON'T THEY, TEMPLE?
ON HIS TOMBSTONE WAS CARVED THE EPITAPH HE WROTE HIMSELF WHEN HE WAS TWENTY-THREE YEARS OLD...
ALL PHILADELPHIA PAID FINAL HOMAGE TO A GREAT AMERICAN...
THE BODY OF BENJAMIN FRANKLIN, PRINTER
(LIKE THE COVER OF AN OLD BOOK, ITS CONTENTS TORN OUT AND STRIPPED OF ITS LETTERING AND GILDING) LIES HERE, FOOD FOR WORMS.
YET THE WORK ITSELF SHALL NOT BE LOST, FOR IT WILL, AS HE BELIEVED, APPEAR ONCE MORE IN A NEW AND MORE ELEGANT EDITION REVISED AND CORRECTED BY THE AUTHOR.

## Benjamin Franklin (1706 - 1790)

Portrait of Benjamin Franklin by Joseph Duplessis (c. 1785)

**INTRODUCTION**

By William B. Jones Jr.

Author of *Classics Illustrated: A Cultural History*

Of all the Founding Fathers of the United States of America, Benjamin Franklin (1706-1790) is in many ways the most approachable. George Washington seems too austere, Thomas Jefferson too cerebral, John Adams too irritable, Alexander Hamilton too calculating, and so forth. But "B. Franklin, Printer" - the witty, practical, self-made man who tamed lightning and charmed the ladies of Versailles - is another matter altogether. His appealing persona, carefully crafted in the pages of his *Autobiography*, draws us toward him across the centuries, with a waggish glint in those eyes behind the bifocals he invented.

It goes without saying that Franklin is so many other things, as well. He, along with Jefferson, embodied the Enlightenment in America. If the eighteenth century was the Age of Reason, he was Reason personified and domesticated, a home-grown "philosophe" (as the French would say) and man of science. As Sculley Bradley observed, "it was Franklin's particular genius to make the rational life comprehensible and practicable to his countrymen" (*The American Tradition in Literature*, 4th ed., p. 111). He carried out this project through vehicles as different as *Poor Richard's Almanack*, the meetings of the Junto club in Philadelphia, his treatise *Experiments and Observations on Electricity*, and the founding of the nonsectarian University of Pennsylvania.

Other achievements and contributions to the common weal included the first American circulating library (the Library Company of Philadelphia), the first American hospital (the Pennsylvania Hospital), and the first American scholarly institute (the American Philosophical Society). Among his inventions were the Franklin stove, the lightning rod, a storage battery, and a musical instrument, the glass harmonica, for which Mozart composed and on which Marie Antoinette played. Franklin served in a variety of capacities in civic life, from clerk of the Pennsylvania Assembly to colonial agent in London for Pennsylvania, Georgia, Massachusetts and New Jersey. As a member of the Second Continental Congress, he served with Jefferson and Adams on the committee charged with drafting the Declaration of Independence.

Representing the new nation as a diplomat in France, the elder statesman became the greatest celebrity of the day and a particular favourite with stylish younger

***Cont'd***

women, who began wearing wigs styled after his fur cap. "To the French," biographer Walter Isaacson writes, "this lightning-defying scientist and tribune of liberty who had unexpectedly appeared on their shores was a symbol both of the virtuous frontier freedom romanticised by Rousseau and of the Enlightenment's reasoned wisdom championed by Voltaire" (*Benjamin Franklin*, pp. 325-6). Franklin spent nine years at Passy, near Paris, enjoying the enraptured attention of fashionable society (much to the disgust of John Adams), writing the delightful "Bagatelles," and, incidentally, forging the alliance that won the War of American Independence.

After having secured the Treaty of Paris that ended the conflict, he returned to Philadelphia, nearing the age of eighty. But retirement was out of the question. Once again, Franklin was called to public service, first as president of the executive council of Pennsylvania and then as a delegate to the Constitutional Convention of 1787. He took an active part in the deliberations, proposing a crucial compromise that led to the definition of the roles of the United States Senate and House of Representatives. At the conclusion of the proceedings, as fellow delegates signed the national charter, he pointed to the sun carved on the back of convention president George Washington's chair and said, "I have often in the course of the session, and the vicissitudes of my hopes and fears as to its issue, looked at that behind the President without being able to tell whether it was rising or setting. But now at length I have the happiness to know that it is a rising and not a setting sun."

Franklin is buried in Philadelphia at Christ (Episcopal) Church beside his wife, Deborah, who first saw him on that day in 1723 when the nearly penniless printer's apprentice, newly arrived from Boston, "went up Market Street," encumbered with "three great puffy rolls." His humane, inquisitive, entrepreneurial spirit remains alive in the city and nation he helped to build. Successive generations have discovered and delighted in his pithy epigrams, which contain equal measures of wit and wisdom: "One today is worth two tomorrows"; "Three may keep a secret if two of them are dead"; "Necessity never made a good bargain"; "There never was a good war or a bad peace"; "In this world nothing can be said to be certain, except death and taxes"; "Human felicity is produced not so much by great pieces of good fortune that seldom happen, as by little advantages that occur every day."

Portrait of Benjamin Franklin in London by David Martin (1767)

## Benjamin Franklin's Quotes

There are a number of famous quotes that have been attributed to Benjamin Franklin. Below is a selection of favourites.

*"By failing to prepare, you are preparing to fail."*

*"They who can give up essential liberty to obtain a little temporary safety deserve neither liberty nor safety."*

*"Wine is constant proof that God loves us and loves to see us happy."*

*"Never leave that till tomorrow which you can do today."*

*"There never was a good war or a bad peace."*

*"We are all born ignorant, but one must work hard to remain stupid."*

*"A penny saved is a penny earned."*

*"Genius without education is like silver in the mine."*

*"He that is good for making excuses is seldom good for anything else."*

*"Never ruin an apology with an excuse."*

*"Love your Enemies, for they tell you your faults."*

*"If you desire many things, many things will seem but a few."*

*"Distrust & caution are the parents of security."*

*"Mankind naturally and generally love to be flatter'd."*

*"If all printers were determined not to print anything till they were sure it would offend nobody, there would be very little printed."*

*"Remember that time is money."*

**Did you know...**

*Benjamin Franklin invented many things that are still in wide use today. Here is a list of some of them:*

- *Bifocals*
- *The Lightning Rod*
- *The Franklin Stove*
- *Swim Fins (like flippers, but worn on the hands)*
- *The Glass Armonica (also known as the glass harmonica)*
- *Flexible Urinary Catheter*
- *Odometer*
- *The "Long Arm", for reaching things in high places.*

**Did you know...**

*Benjamin Franklin stands alone as the only person to have signed all four of the documents which helped to create the United States of America: the Declaration of Independence (1776); the Treaty of Alliance, Amity, and Commerce with France (1778); the Treaty of Peace between England, France, and the United States (1782); and the US Constitution (1787). He also helped to write parts of the Declaration of Independence and the US Constitution!*